XXXG-00W0
WING GUNDAM ZERO [E

XXXG-00W0
WING GUNDAM ZERO [EW]

ZECHS

That thing was hand-made?

TREIZE

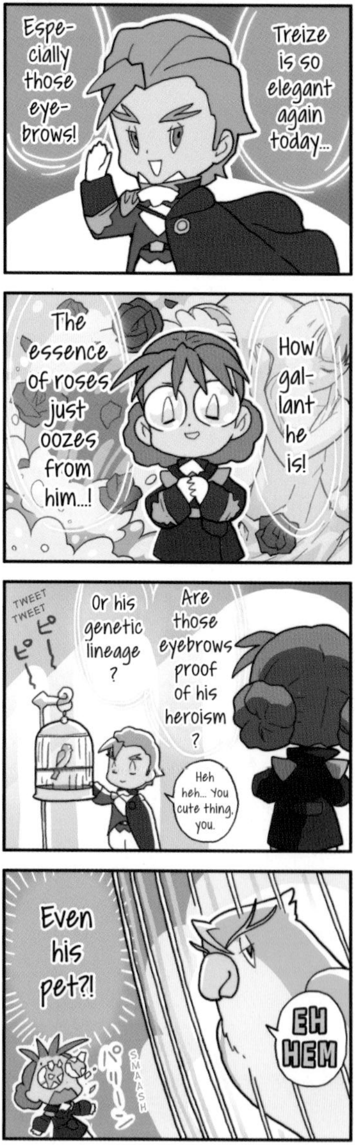
Treize is so elegant again today...
Especially those eyebrows!
The essence of roses just oozes from him...!
How gallant he is!
Are those eyebrows proof of his heroism?
Or his genetic lineage?
TWEET
TWEET
Heh heh... You cute thing, you.
Even his pet?!
SMAASH
EH HEM

Mobile Suit GUNDAM WING Endless Waltz Glory of the Losers 13

Story

Katsuyuki Sumizawa

Art

Tomofumi Ogasawara

CONTENTS

OUTLINE

In A.C. 195, tensions climb to volatile heights between Earth and the space colonies. Treize is reinstated as OZ Commander-in-Chief and declares do-or-die war against White Fang, led by Zechs (Milliardo). Meanwhile in space, Colony C-00421, where Trowa is living, is invaded by remnants of OZ's space military forces. Trowa retrieves the Gundam Heavyarms from Heero and Sally and sorties in it. Learning that Colony C-00421 has been seized, Zechs gives the order to fire Space Fortress Libra's main cannon on it. Relena risks her life to try to stop her brother Zechs, but he does not waver in his resolve. However, learning that the colony has been liberated, he now gives the order to fire on the Romefeller Foundation headquarters on Earth. Relena fears the worst possible outcome. Then Dorothy appears and says that she and Relena want to be by Zech's side so this "final war" can be burned into their eyes. Zechs accepts Dorothy's request, and the pair are escorted onto the Libra.

Chapter 75 "EVE WARS I: G Team, Sortie!!"
G TEAM, ASSEMBLE ON THE BRIDGE!
G TEAM, ASSEMBLE ON THE BRIDGE!

THIS IS THE QUIET BEFORE THE STORM.
IT WOULD SEEM THAT BOTH ENEMY ARMIES HAVE BEEN TAKING UP POSITIONS DURING THIS TIME.
BUT SO HAVE WE.
I'VE FINISHED REFITTING THE HEAVYARMS AND SANDROCK FOR USE IN SPACE.
I'VE ALSO USED ARCHITECTURE BACKUPS TO SUCCESSFULLY RESTORE THE WING ZERO SYSTEMS THAT HAD LOST FUNCTIONALITY.
I'VE ALSO FINISHED FINE-TUNING A NEWLY-MADE SHIELD FOR IT AS WELL.

NOW THEN, WHAT'LL YOU DO, EH?
YOU CAN ALL SORTIE AS THE "G TEAM" AT ANY TIME.

EARTH?
OR WHITE FANG?
WHICH SIDE WILL YOU TAKE?
NEI-THER!
WE'LL TAKE DOWN TREIZE AND ZECHS BOTH!

I LIKE IT. THERE'S NO PRECEDENT OF A TWO-FRONT BATTLE BEING SUCCESSFUL. IT'S A POOR PLAN.
I WON'T CHOOSE SUCH A STUPID PLAN. THE KEY TO SUCCESS OF ANY STRATEGY IS CONCENTRATING YOUR FIGHTING POWER.
IT'S THE STRATEGY THAT'S BEST SUITED TO US GUYS WHO KEEP LOSING, I FIGURE.
FIRST WE'LL HIT LIBRA WITH ALL WE'VE GOT! THEN WE'LL HIT TREIZE!
SFF
BUT THE QUESTION REMAINS OF WHETHER WE ACTUALLY CAN.

WELL, WE CAN'T VERY WELL JUST LEAVE LIBRA BE...
I VOTE WITH WUFEI.
...SO WE'LL BE FIGHTING AGAINST ZECHS?
THAT DUDE IS DEAD SERIOUS.
BUT IF HE'S FIGHTING FOR THE COLO-NIES, THEN...
WHOA, WHOA! DO YOU STILL THINK HE'S ON OUR SIDE?

MILLIARDO THINKS OF US AS HIS ENEMIES.
THERE'S NO ROOM FOR NEGO-TIATING WITH HIM.
...
HEERO, WHAT'S YOUR OPINION ?

WHO'S GOING TO TAKE COM-MAND?
I THINK WUFEI WOULD BE PERFECT.
IF IT'S US HE'S LEADING ...
THEN WHAT WE NEED IS WUFEI'S COOL JUDGMENT AND STRONG LEADERSHIP.

IF YOU AID ME AS ADVISER.
OF COURSE! I'D DO SO WITH PLEASURE.
WELL, THEN I WILL ACCEPT.
IN THAT CASE, I WILL FOLLOW YOUR ORDERS, WUFEI.
I'M A TOOL OF WAR. I HAVE NO RIGHT TO STATE OPINIONS.

WELP! THAT'S ALL DECIDED THEN!
SO THEY'RE GOING TO FIGHT AGAINST BOTH THE EARTH AND WHITE FANG?
THESE FOOLS ARE ALL SUICIDAL MANIACS.

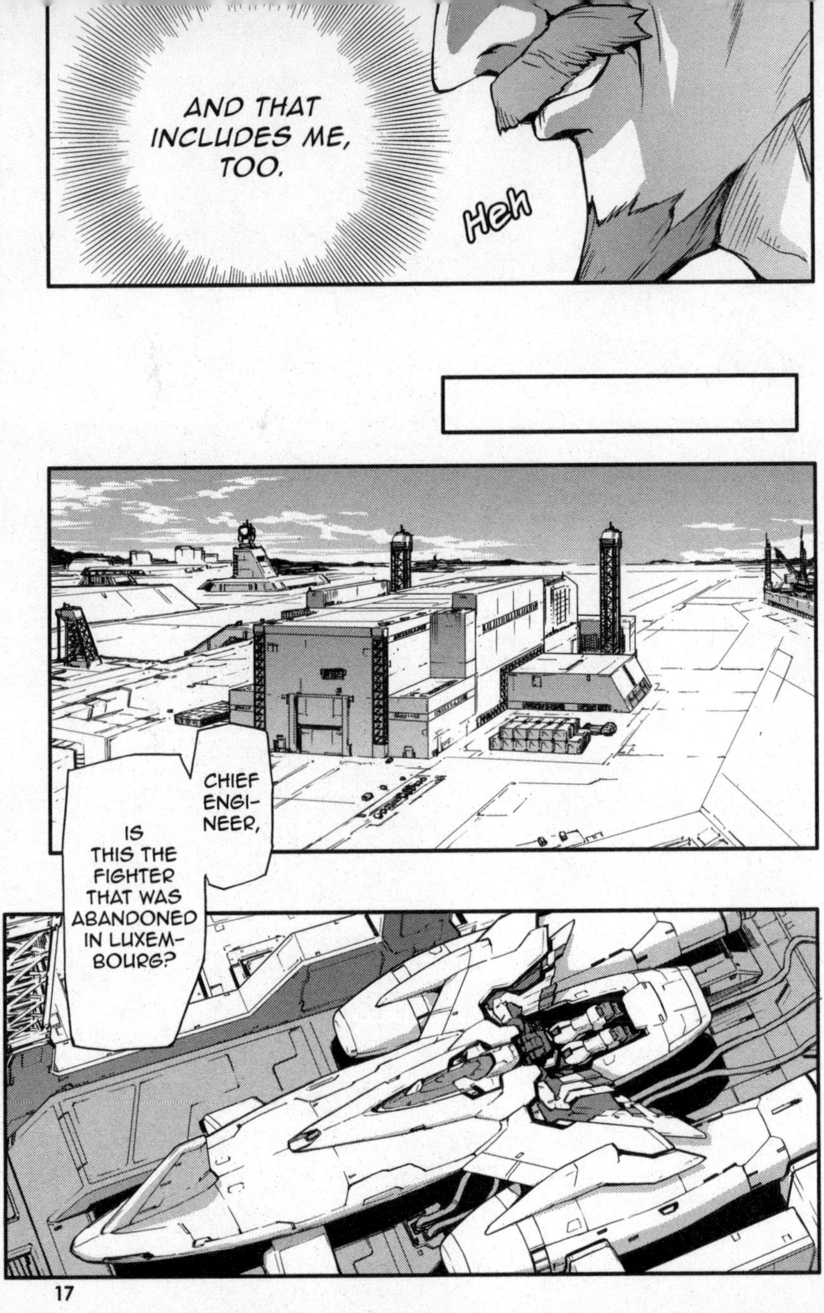
AND THAT INCLUDES ME, TOO.
Heh
CHIEF ENGI-NEER,
IS THIS THE FIGHTER THAT WAS ABANDONED IN LUXEM-BOURG?

YES... IT'S A SPLENDID FIGHTER, THOUGH.
BUT HIS EXCEL-LENCY TREIZE HAS GONE OFF TO SPACE.
WHAT'S THE POINT OF ATTACHING BOOSTERS TO THIS THING NOW?
WE CAN'T JUST DUMP IT WHEN IT'S PAR-TIALLY COM-PLETE.
SOMEDAY THE TIME WILL COME WHEN IT BECOMES USEFUL...
STILL ...
THERE AREN'T ANY PILOTS LEFT ON EARTH THAT COULD FLY A FIGHTER LIKE THIS.

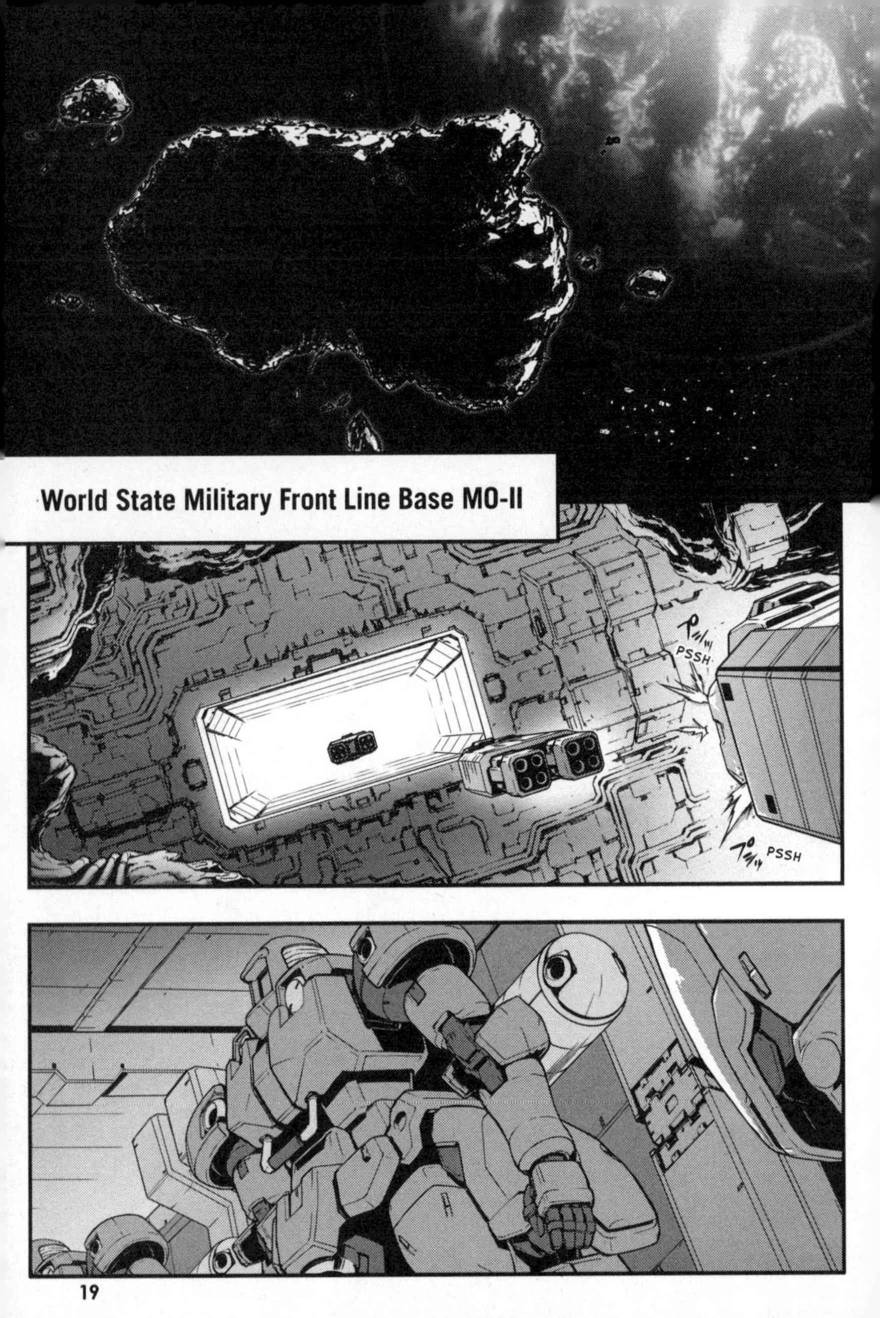
World State Military Front Line Base MO-II
PSSH
PSSH

Treize Khushrenada, head of the World State, built up battalions of thousands of armored Mobile Suits—the latest-model Leos—as his main military force at MO-II, the resource satellite closest to Earth.
Treize declared that he would lead the vanguard himself, and the fighting morale of the troops was whipped up to new heights, but some skepticism about how much resistance MS units could put up against a gigantic battleship remained.

GONG
GWOOM
GONG
FIGHTING IS THE ONLY THING THAT CAN END FIGHTING.

THE ONLY ONES THAT UNDERSTAND THAT HERE IN SPACE...
ARE MILLIARDO AND MYSELF.

VWOOOOOOO

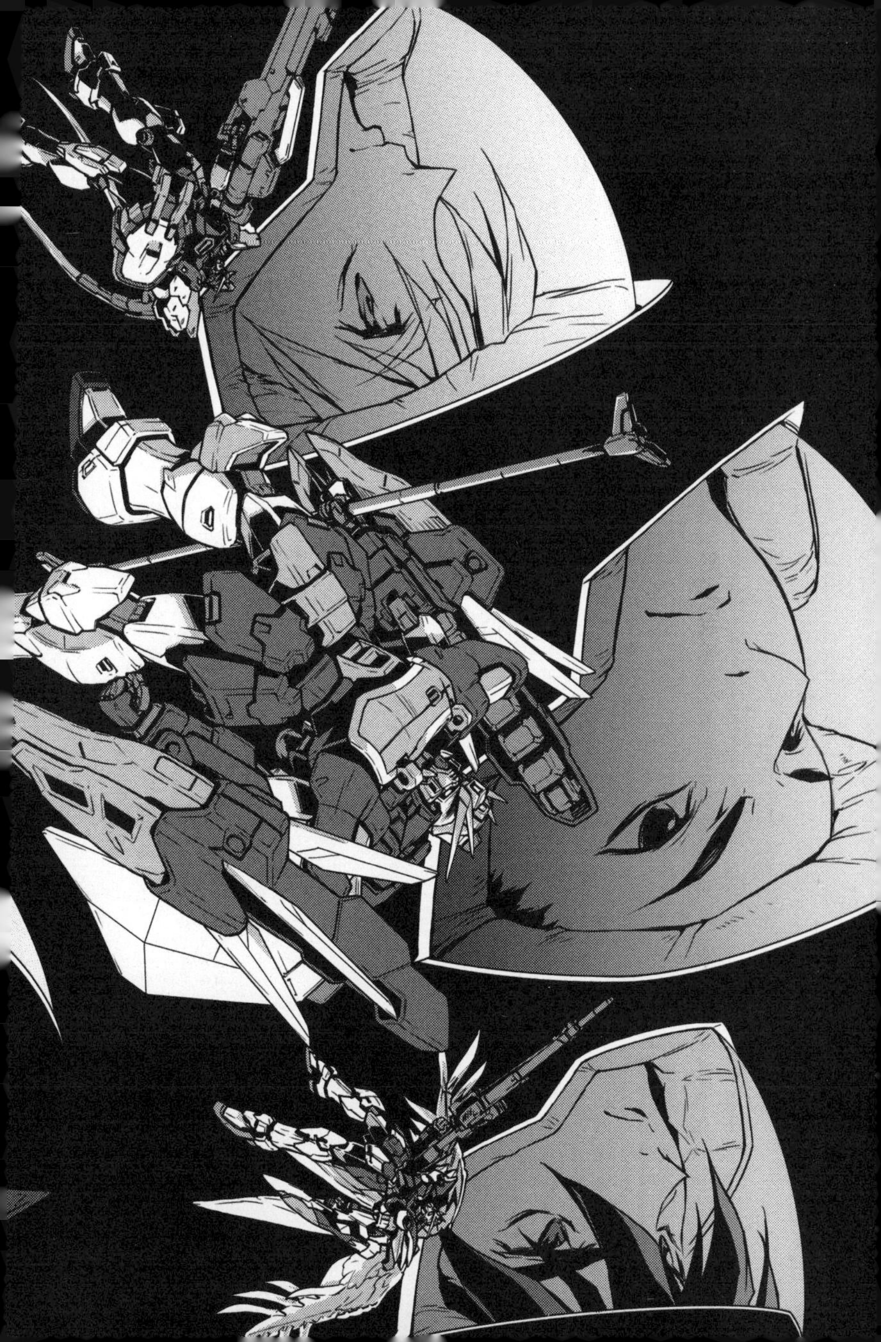

THE ONLY THING BORN FROM FIGHTING IS MORE FIGHTING.
PEACE REQUIRES KINDNESS WHICH SEVERS THOSE CHAINS OF HATRED.
OFFENSE IS THE GREATEST DEFENSE.
IF YOU THINK OF NOTHING BUT BEING ON GUARD, YOU BECOME PARALYZED!

GONG
GWOOM
GWOOM
GWOOM

THMP
...
WHAT THE ...?!

RO-SYSTEM ▷▷▷ LOADING ▷▷▷ ZERO
THE GUNDAM EPYON'S ZERO SYSTEM IS BEING DOWNLOADED INTO THE CONTROL SYSTEM OF THE NEW-MODEL VIRGOS!!
WHEN IT FINISHES, THE MDS WILL BECOME THE ULTIMATE FIGHTING TROOPS...
ALERT
Condition
ondition : RED
VREEEET
VREEEET
ENEMY AS-SAULT!
ENEMY AS-SAULT!

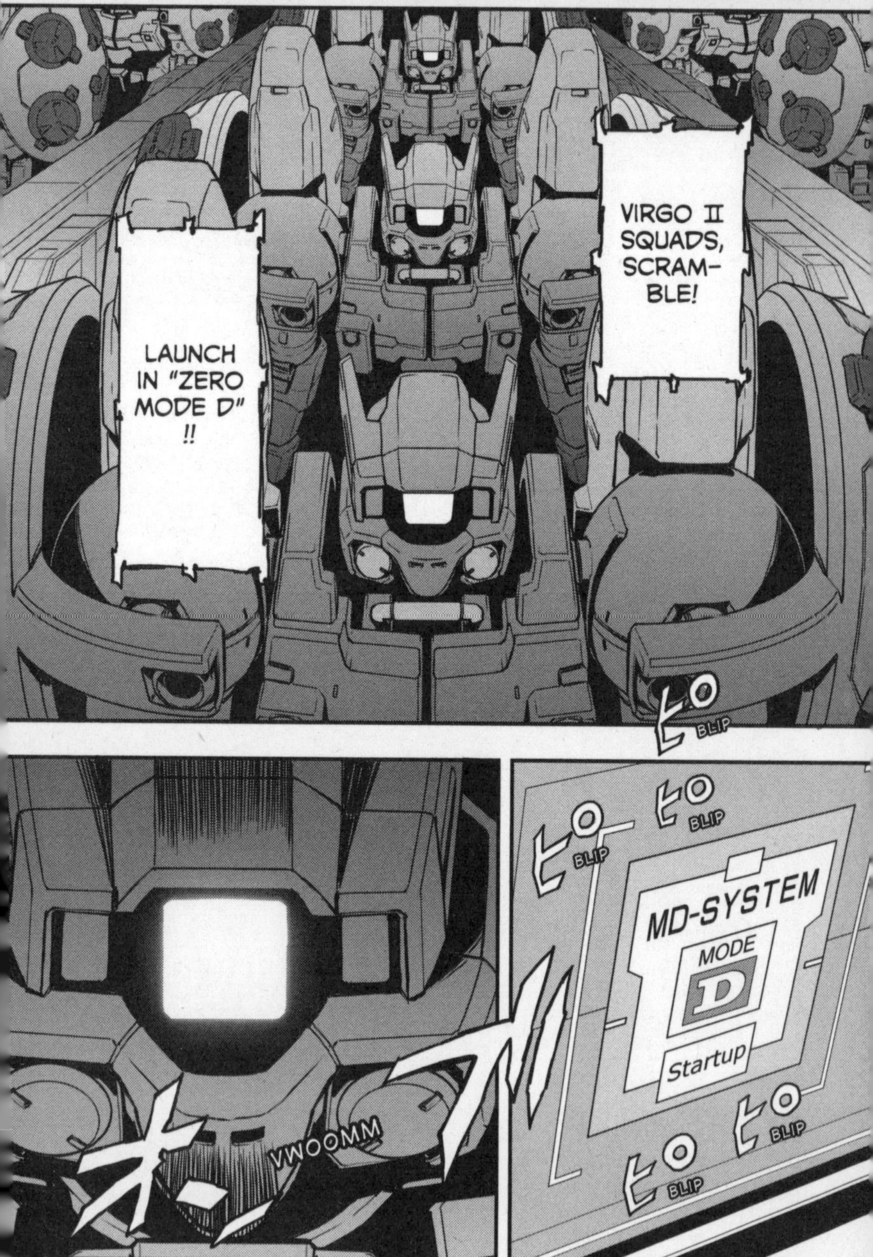
VIRGO II SQUADS, SCRAM-BLE!
LAUNCH IN "ZERO MODE D" !!
BLIP
BLIP
BLIP
MD-SYSTEM
MODE
D
Startup
BLIP
BLIP
VWOOMM

DOOM
DOOM
DOOM
DOOM
DOOM
DOOM
OOOOOOOOOOO

Duo *Maxwell*

SLEEVE NOTES:
Endless Waltz

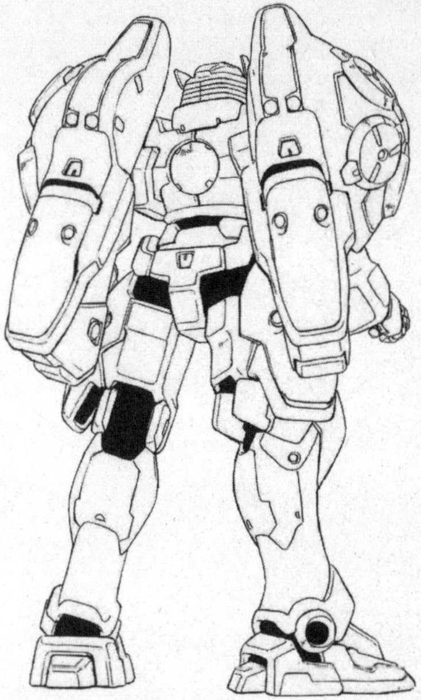

WF-02MD
VIRGO II

Enhanced model of the Virgos that were being developed at OZ's moon base. White Fang commandeered the fighters which had been left behind at the moon base, finished them and deployed them in the EVE WARS. They are equipped with six Planet Defensors and enhanced armaments. Furthermore, with the ZERO System installed, operations can be performed in which clusters are controlled en masse.

BACKPACK AND MEGA BEAM CANNON

The added backpack is mounted on the shoulder armor. The backpack with main thrusters can also house a Beam Rifle, and the Mega Beam Cannon is connected to the shoulder via a cable.

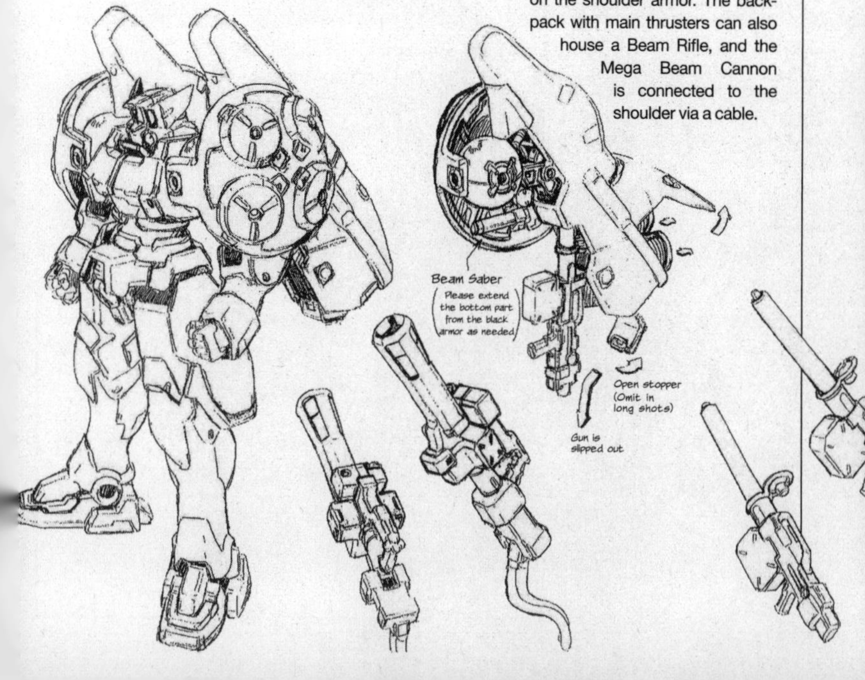

VWOOOO
A NEW-MODEL VIRGO SQUAD ?! AND...
IT'S A HUGE SWARM !!
Chapter 76 "EVE WARS II: ZERO MODE"
[WF] TYPE VIRGO
BIP
BIP
BIP
BIP
G5
G1
G2
G3
G4

WOW... THAT'S QUITE A LOT OF THEM, HUH...

THAT'S HOW AFRAID OF US THEY ARE.
LET'S FAN OUT OR THEY'LL DROWN US IN CONCENTRATED FIRE-POWER!

WE RAN OUT OF TIME... WE DIDN'T HAVE A CHANCE TO EQUIP THAT GEAR...
SO I'LL JUST HAVE TO FIGHT WITH ALL THE POWER I DO HAVE!
PLEASE TARGET THE CENTRAL AREA WHERE THE SQUADS ARE CONCEN-TRATED!
JA KANG
ROGER THAT...
VWM
BAKUNG
GREEEEM
VWM

GRAA
CHOO
OOOM
BAM

VWOOOSH
NO WAY!
LOOKS LIKE THE MOBILE DOLLS HAVE BEEN LOADED WITH SOME KIND OF TACTICAL PROGRAM.
THEY ANTICIPATED OUR ATTACK... THAT'S THE WAY ZERO MOVES.

SO THINGS AREN'T THE WAY THEY WERE BEFORE, HUH?
ZECHS IS PUSHING FOR A WAR OF ATTRITION.
HE'LL JUST KEEP THROWING UNITS AT US UNTIL WE'VE WORN OURSELVES OUT.
WE'LL TEACH HIM THAT DOLING OUT HIS MILITARY POWER LIKE THIS IS A STUPID TACTIC!

VWOMM
DON
DON
DON
DON
BYOOM
BWA
BAMM

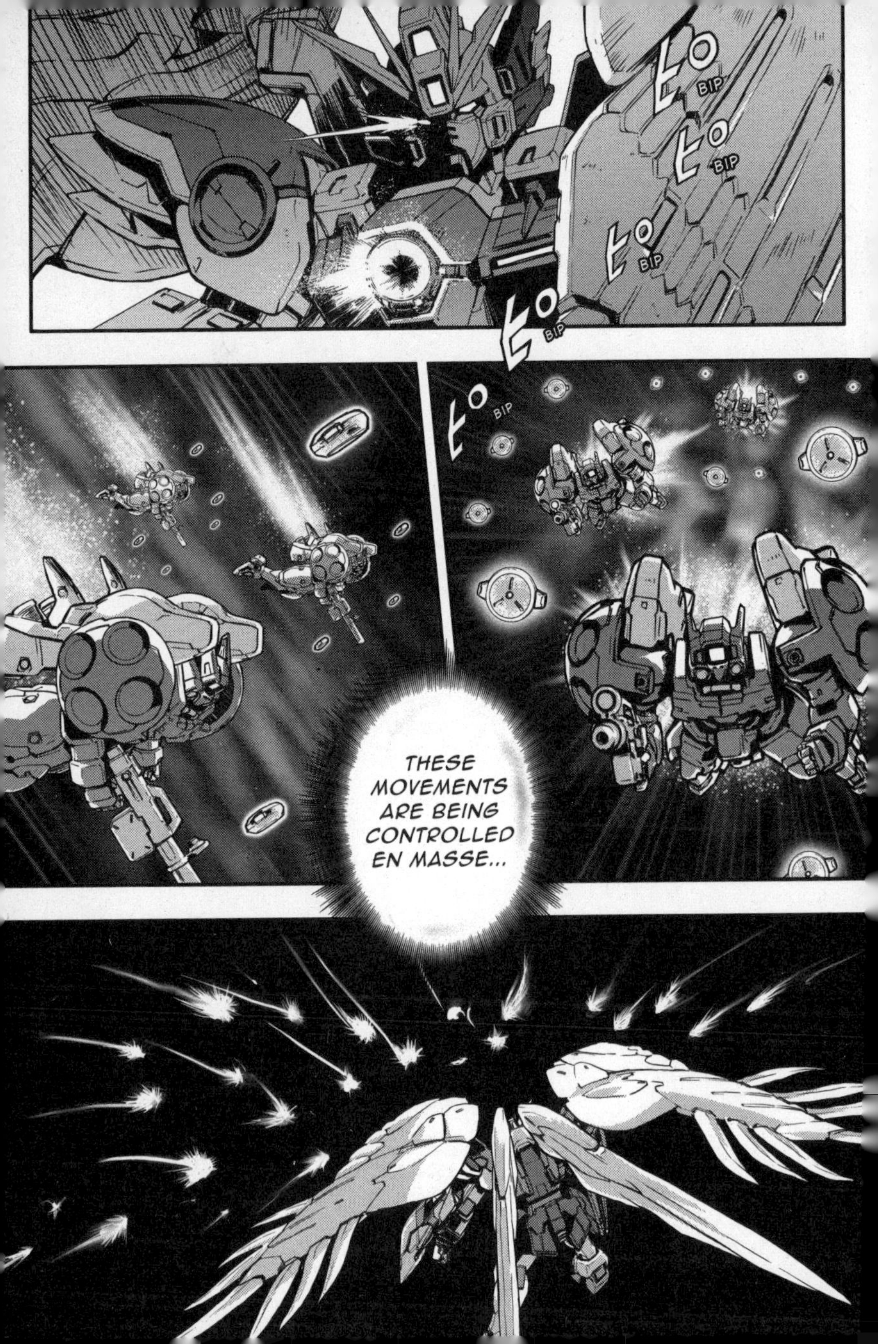
BIP
BIP
BIP
BIP
BIP
THESE MOVEMENTS ARE BEING CONTROLLED EN MASSE...

VWOO
OOOO
I KNOW, ZERO...
WE CAN'T BEAT ZECHS AT THIS RATE.

THE EARTH AS SEEN FROM SPACE IS BEAUTIFUL ...
THE ONLY ONES WHO UNDERSTAND AND LOVE THIS TRUE BEAUTY ARE THE RESIDENTS OF THE SPACE HABITATS.
THESE FEELINGS OF BOTH ENVY AND REVERENCE ARE IN A PLACE THAT PEOPLE STANDING ON THE EARTH ITSELF CAN NEVER REACH.
THAT'S WHY THE PEOPLE OF THE COLONIES— I MEAN, THE SPACE HABITATS— YEARN FOR PEACE WITH ALL THEIR HEARTS,
AND I THINK THAT THEY COULD HAVE BEEN ABLE TO BUILD A DEMILITAR-IZED, NON-VIOLENT WORLD.

EH HEH HEH! BUT THE TRUTH IS, ALL THEY'VE DONE IS RUN FROM WAR.
THEY LAZE AWAY ALL WARM AND SNUG IN THE FALSE PEACE CONTROLLED BY THE ALLIANCE ARMY.
ON THAT SCORE, THE GUNDAM PILOTS ARE MARVELOUS!
FLIT
THEY'RE NOBLE-MINDED KNIGHTS THAT FIGHT WITH PASSION AND FEROCITY,
PROUDLY INDEPEN-DENT WARRIORS,
AND THEY CONTINUE TO BE GLORIOUS LOSERS.

THUP
!
BRO-
THER!
WHUD
COMMANDER MILLIARDO, THE DESTRUCTIVE POWER OF THE WING ZERO IS FAR BEYOND WHAT WE ANTICIPATED.

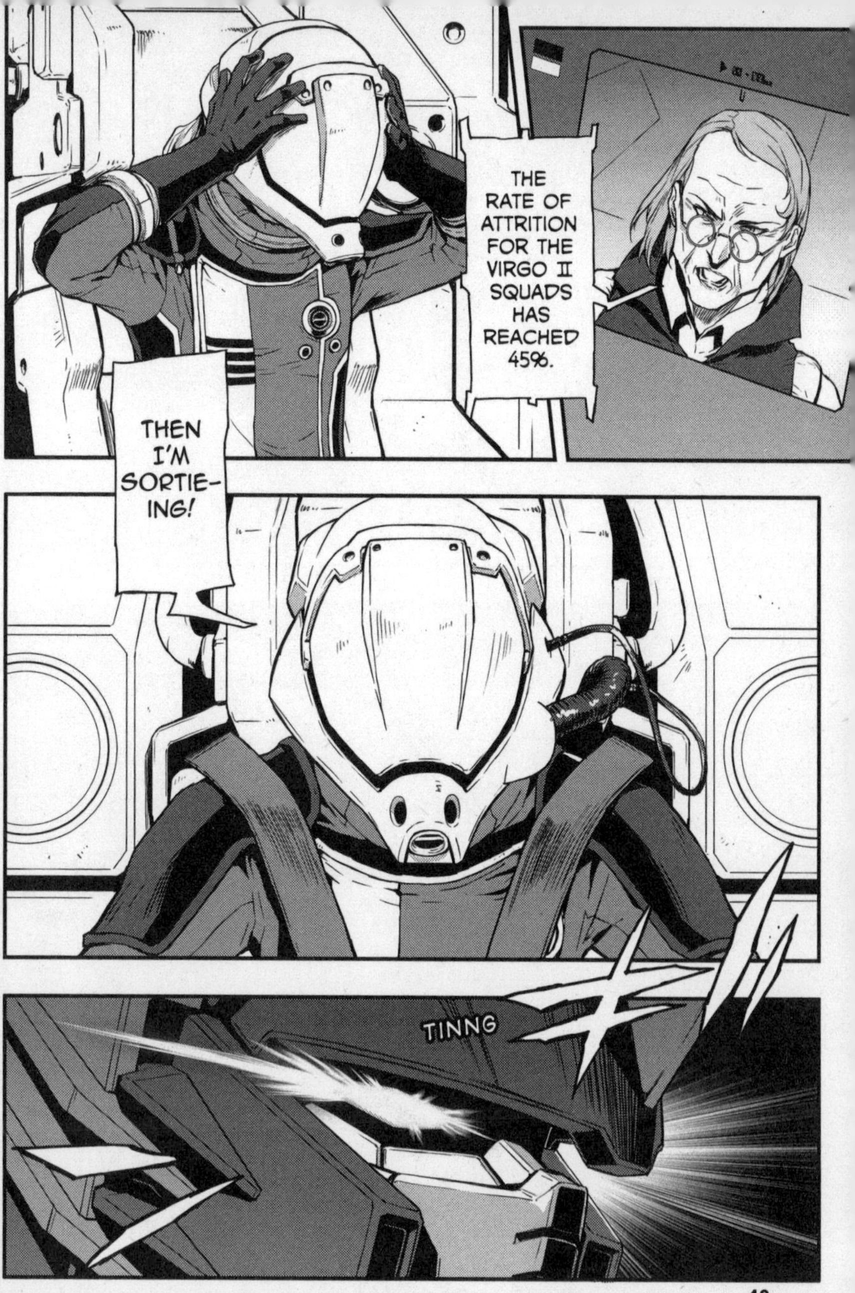
THE RATE OF ATTRITION FOR THE VIRGO II SQUADS HAS REACHED 45%.
THEN I'M SORTIE-ING!
TINNG

OPEN
BLIP
BLIP
BLIP
BLIP
GO RIGHT IN, MISS RELENA.
KSSH
THIS IS THE CONTROL ROOM WHERE COMMANDS ARE SENT TO THE MOBILE DOLLS USING THE ZERO SYSTEM.
MD SYSTEM
STANDBY
IT'S A SPECIAL SYSTEM, SO I DON'T RECOMMEND YOU USE IT, MISS RELENA,
BUT I HAVE A VERY GOOD AFFINITY WITH IT.
I HAVE TREIZE'S STAMP OF AP-PROVAL.
...
MILLIARDO SAW THE DATA AND WAS QUITE SURPRISED ...
HEH HEH !
HOW IT PLEASES ME TO BE ABLE TO BE OF ASSISTANCE TO MILLIARDO !

WATCH. BY USING THIS SYSTEM, THOSE BLOODLESS DOLLS WILL BECOME ABLE TO MOVE ACCORDING TO THE WILL OF A HUMAN.
THEY WILL BE ELEVATED FROM DOLLS TO MARIO-NETTES!
VIRGO II NUMBER 2 SQUAD, STANDBY!
STARTUP IN "ZERO MODE M" !!
MD-SYSTEM
MODE
M
Startup
YOU'RE REALLY GOING TO CONTROL THEM?
YES... IT'S THE ONLY WAY FOR ME TO SURVIVE ON THIS SHIP.

WHY DID YOU BRING ME HERE?
I THOUGHT I WOULD SHOW YOU THE ONE WAY TO STOP THIS WAR, MISS RELENA.
KTNK
USE THIS AND SHOOT ME DEAD.
THAT WILL HALT THE SYSTEM.
?!
DOROTHY ?!

VWWOO

OOOO
OOOO

ゴ DUN
ゴ DUN
ゴ DUN
ゴ DUN
ゴ DUN
ゴッ
VWOOOH
ズォ
!
ピ BIP
ピ BIP
ピ BIP
ピ BIP
ピ BIP

CHOOM
BWOOSH
HEERO! WHERE ARE YOU GOING ?!
THE EPYON IS COMING !
I HAVE TO TAKE HIM ON!
GAGUNK
HEERO, DON'T LEAVE! WE NEED THE ZERO SYSTEM AND YOUR FIREPOWER HERE!
KINK
GWOOM
CHAK

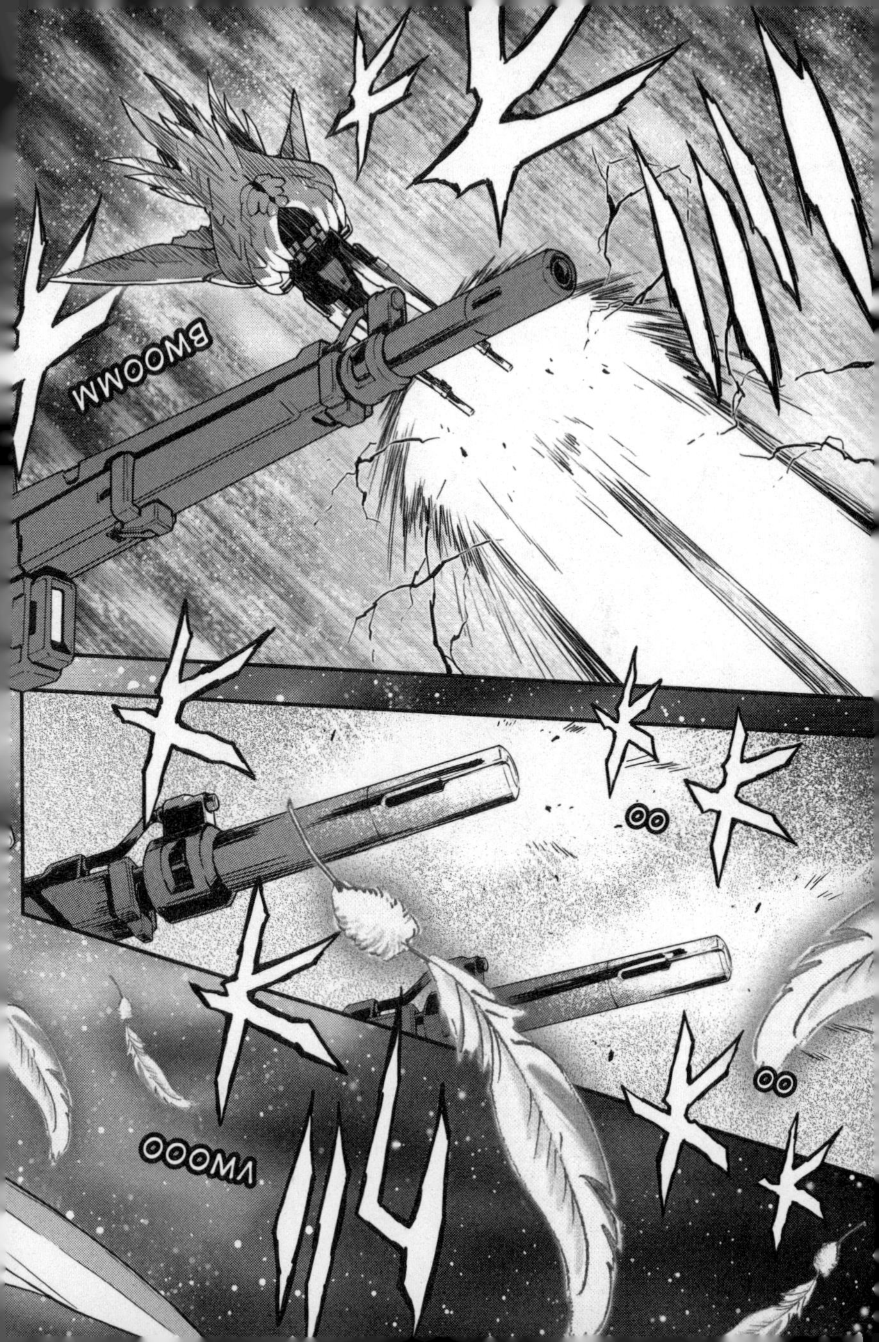
BWOOMM
VWOOO

DOOM
DOOM
DOOM
DOOM
DOOM
DOOM
VOOOSH
DON'T WORRY. THE ZERO SYSTEM'S IN YOUR GUNDAM, TOO.

IN THE SANDROCK ?!
I ASKED HOWARD TO DO IT...
THE SYSTEM WILL ACTIVATE WITH "CODE ZERO."
I CAN'T! I CAN'T HANDLE THE ZERO!
I'M NOT ...
I'M NOT QUALIFIED !!
DO IT.
IT WILL BE YOUR ATONEMENT TO SPACE.
HEERO ...

VWOM
GAKINK
HERE THEY COME!!
BYOOM
NOW, MY LITTLE MARIO-NETTES!
DANCE A LOVELY WALTZ FOR ME!
chik

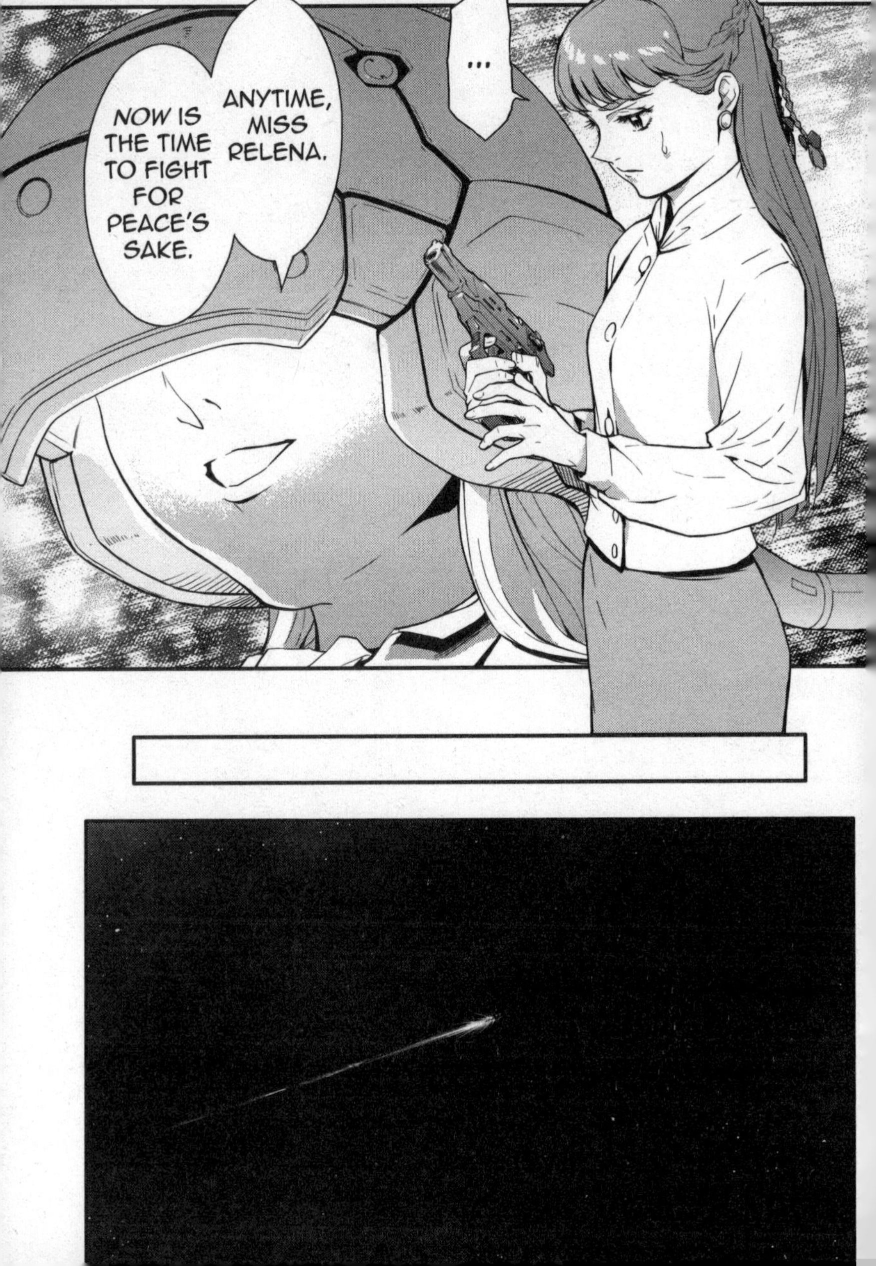
...
ANYTIME, MISS RELENA.
NOW IS THE TIME TO FIGHT FOR PEACE'S SAKE.

BIP
BIP
SO, YOU'VE ARRIVED ... HEERO YUY!
BIP
BIP
BIP
ZECHS!
TELL ME YOUR TRUE MOTIVES!

ZWAM
YOU WERE BORN ON EARTH, SO WHY ARE YOU FIGHTING FOR THE COLONIES ?!
YOU DISAPPROVE?! IN THAT CASE, YOU, WHO WERE BORN IN A HABITAT, SHOULD TAKE COMMAND OF WHITE FANG !!
DAZWAM

OR AT LEAST BECOME MY BROTHER-IN-ARMS!!
...

WF-02MD

VIRGO II

SLEEVE NOTES:
Endless Waltz

MEGA SPACE BATTLESHIP LIBRA

A massive battleship originally constructed by the Romefeller Foundation to place the Earth Sphere under its control. White Fang captured it and made it their flagship. The four rhombus sections are connected in a petal-like arrangement, and the main cannon is located in the central block. It is powerful enough to destroy a colony or a city on the Earth with a single blast.

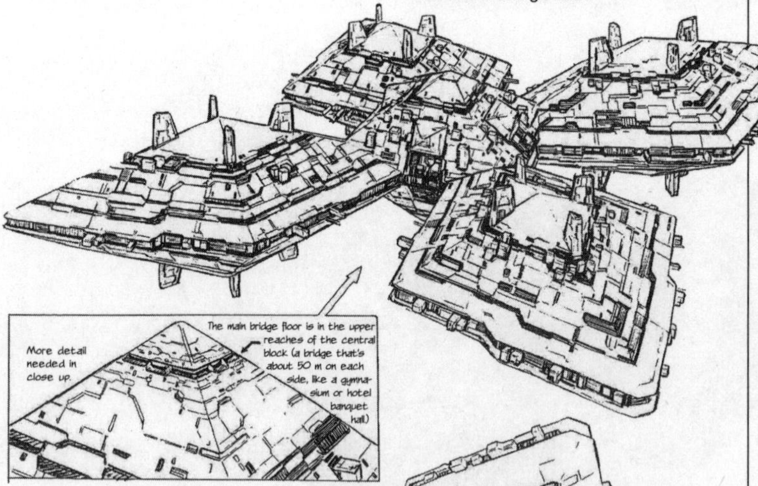
The main bridge floor is in the upper reaches of the central block (a bridge that's about 50 m on each side, like a gymnasium or hotel banquet hall)
More detail needed in close up.

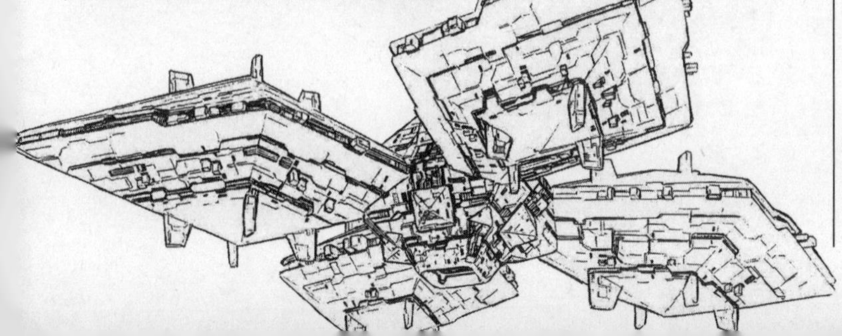

Chapter 77 “EVE WARS III: Breakthrough into Darkness”

BYOOM
GRA
WOOO

THE GUNDAM EPYON— THE NEXT MECHA— IS FOR LOSERS TO PILOT.
I THINK YOU CAN SEE IT, ZECHS...
A VISION OF YOU DE-STROYING THE EARTH!
FLASH

BOOM
BOOM
BOOM
BOOM
BOOM
...
EVEN IF I KNOW I'M GOING TO LOSE, I HAVE NO CHOICE BUT TO KEEP FIGHTING IN ORDER TO END THIS!

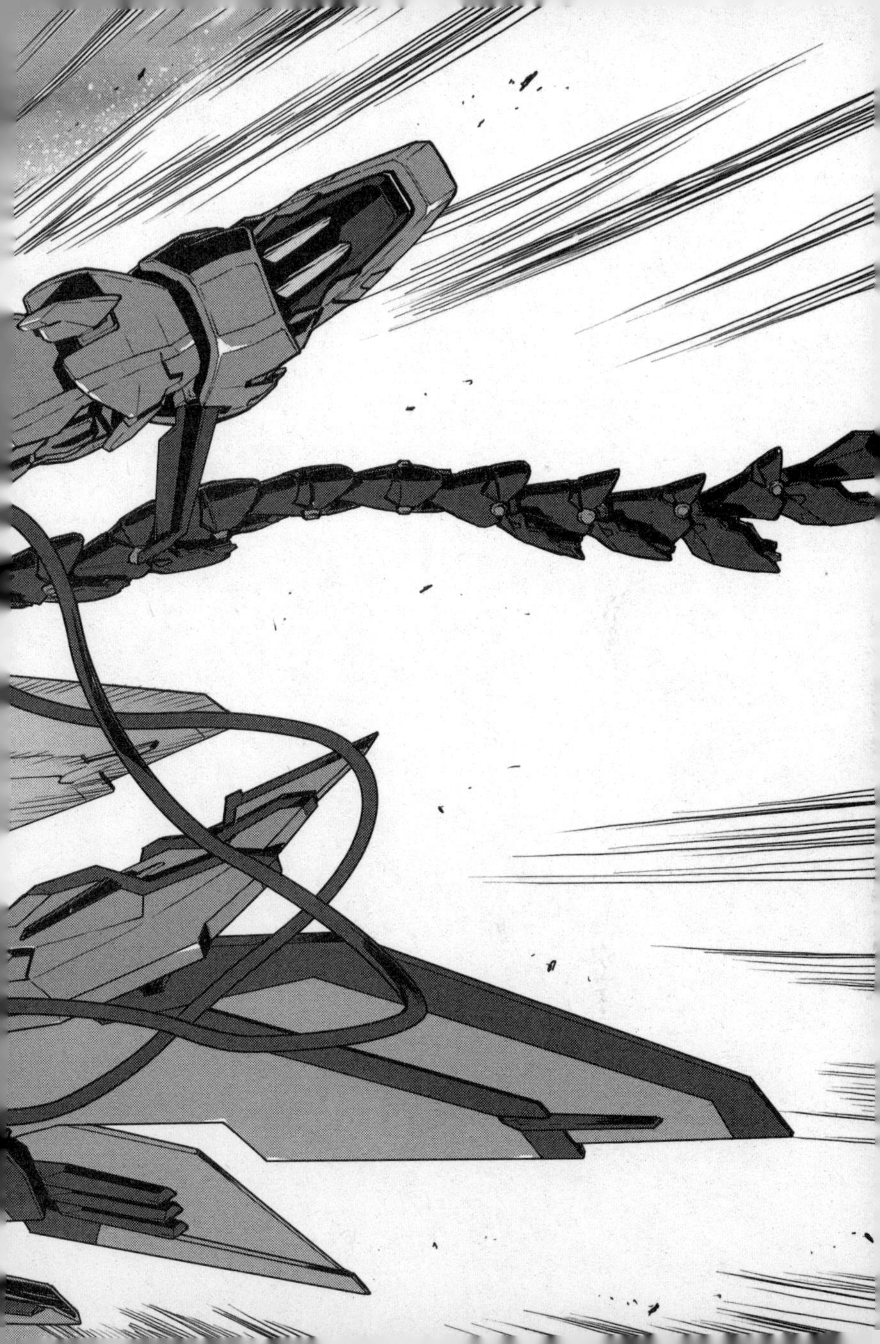

ZWABAM
BSSHT
BAM
BAWOOM

ZWA
BAM
NGH!
BAM
BAM
BAM
ZHA
GREEEM
BABOOM
BASSHT

GRA
GRA
GRA
GRA
WAAH!
BAM
DWRR
RRR
RRR
VWOOSH
RRR
RRR
BLIP
BLIP
BLIP
BLIP
BLIP
BLIP
G5
G2
T1
G4
G3
...

URGH !!
QUATRE! WE NEED INSTRUCTIONS!
ARE THERE ANY BREACHES?!
ZWABAM
IN THIS CASE, I FIGURE WE HAVE TO EACH DECIDE WHERE TO MAKE OUR OWN!!
RRR
I'LL CUT MY WAY THROUGH FIRST! EVERYONE FOLLOW ME!!
VWOOOSH

TROWA !!
BAZWOO
BWOM
ZHA
BAM
BAM
BAM
N- NEVER MIND ABOUT ME!
BAM
BAM
HURRY ...
GO !!
BSSHT
GABAM
GONG

BA
BAAAM
GWOOM
TROWAAAA!!

?!
Haa
Haa
Haa
W-WAS THAT A HALLUCI-NATION JUST NOW ...?!
QUATRE! WE NEED INSTRUC-TIONS! ARE THERE ANY BREACHES ?!
IN THIS CASE, I FIGURE WE HAVE TO EACH...

W...
WAIT, PLEASE! I'LL GIVE YOU INSTRUC-TIONS!
IF I DON'T WANT TO MAKE SOMEONE SAD, I JUST HAVE TO DO IT MYSELF!

BLIP
BLIP
BLIP
BLIP
ZERO SYSTEM
EXECUTION
CODE - ****
HEART OF SPACE ...!
TELL ME EVERY-THING.

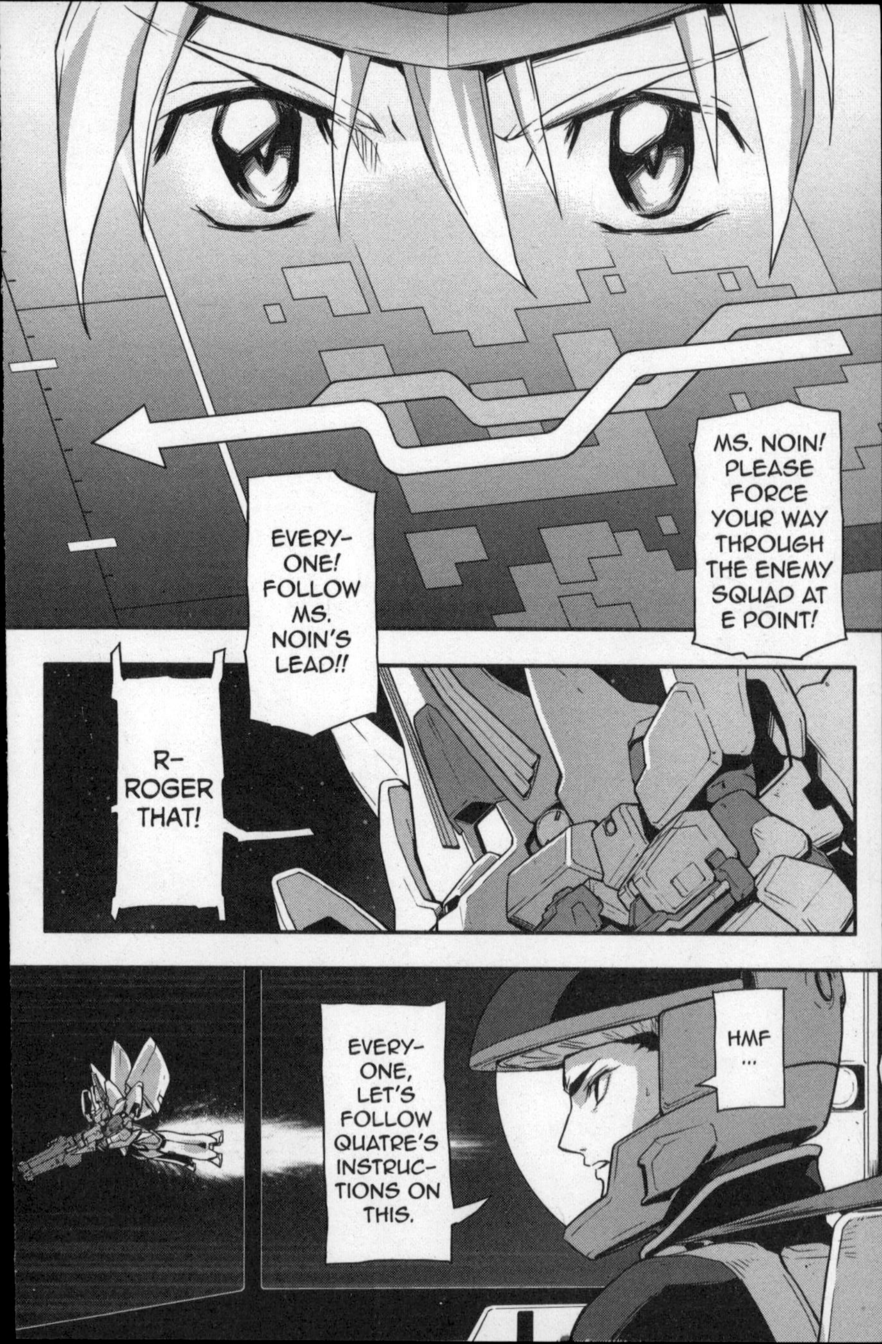
MS. NOIN! PLEASE FORCE YOUR WAY THROUGH THE ENEMY SQUAD AT E POINT!
EVERY-ONE! FOLLOW MS. NOIN'S LEAD!!
R-ROGER THAT!
HMF ...
EVERY-ONE, LET'S FOLLOW QUATRE'S INSTRUC-TIONS ON THIS.

OKAY!
WIL-CO!
VWOMM
BIP
BIP
BIP
BIP
BIP

THE MOBILE DOLLS ARE RE-SPOND-ING
TO A TACTICAL ORDER?
S/TAURUS SK-SDF01A
ENTRY PILOT:LUCREZIA NOIN
A NOIN
ATTACK
SUPPRESSION
"ATTACK SUPPRES-SION" ...
AGAINST LUCREZIA NOIN?!
HEH HEH HEH... HOW VERY KIND-HEARTED MILLIARDO IS...
DID YOU SAY IT'S MS. NOIN?!

!
LUCREZIA NOIN
ATTACK
PERMISSION
ATTACK PERMISSION, EXECUTE !!
BLOCK LIFTED! PRIORITY ON TACTICAL SUPERIORITY!
DOROTHY! STOP!
I CAN'T... LET YOU...
CHKK
SO, IT WOULD SEEM THE SPIRIT'S FINALLY TAKEN HOLD OF YOU, HM?
YES... BUT I CAN'T DO SOMETHING SO LOFTY AS FIGHT FOR PEACE.
ALSO, YOU WERE MY FRIEND ONCE, AND I CAN'T COMMIT AN ACT OF CRUELTY LIKE KILLING YOU.

IN THAT CASE ...
THIS WAR WILL NOT END, WILL IT?
NO.
THIS IS WHAT I'VE BEEN REDUCED TO.
A WOMAN WITH THE BLOOD OF WAR ON MY HANDS, AND IT SUITS ME...

HEERO AND ZECHS SHOULD BE FIGHTING UP AHEAD HERE...
THE ENEMY'S MOVE-MENTS BEFORE FROZE FOR JUST A SECOND.
THEY DID... BUT I DON'T THINK MOBILE DOLLS WOULD HESITATE.
IS A HUMAN MIND OPERAT-ING THE DOLLS?
SOMEBODY IS CHANGING TACTICS IN RESPONSE TO CIRCUM-STANCES!

ZERO... CAN YOU TELL WHAT'S TWO STEPS AHEAD OF US?
VWOOOO
GRAKK
GREEEM

THE FUTURE FOR THE WING ZERO AND THE EPYON HAS NOT CHANGED. THAT IS CERTAIN.
BUT ...
THIS DESTINY OF MINE—TO FAIL—IS CONNECTED TO THE AWAKENING OF MANKIND IN A NEW UNIVERSAL CENTURY IN THE FUTURE!
NO, ZECHS... YOU'RE WRONG! THE ZERO SYSTEM DRAWS CONCLU-SIONS BASED ON THE LOGIC OF THE MIGHTY.
IT CAN'T RESCUE HUMANITY FROM WAR!!
WHO WAS IT THAT TOLD YOU THAT?! THE ZERO SYSTEM ?!
THE MAD SCIENTISTS THAT RAISED YOU PEOPLE ?!
...

VWMM
BWOOMM
YOU GUNDAM PILOTS ARE HURTLING DOWN A TRAJECTORY THAT'S NOT ABOUT HISTORICAL INEVITABILITY OR JUST CAUSE!
THAT'S THE SHAPE YOUR LIVES TAKE— COMBAT PROFES-SIONALS RAISED AS WEAPONS!
...
VWOOM

BYOOMM
YOU'RE NO DIFFERENT THAN THE MOBILE DOLLS HERE!
EXACTLY...
I DON'T DISAGREE.
BLAM

KRAK
AAAAMM
KLATTER
STOP.
YOU CAN'T GET BLOOD ON YOUR HANDS.
Haa
Haa
Haa

WHO ARE YOU ...?
HILDE SCHBEIKER.
I'M A MEMBER OF WHITE FANG NOW...
BUT IN EMOTIONAL TERMS, I FIGURE I'M CLOSE TO THE POSITION OF THE GUNDAM PILOTS.
YOU KNOW THE GUNDAM PILOTS?!
SHKK

CHAK
I CAN'T CON-CEN-TRATE!
COULD YOU TWO BE SO KIND AS TO LEAVE?
MISS DOROTHY!
SFF
CHK
YOUR ARISTO-CRATIC GAMES END HERE!!
KTINK
BMF
WEEEEEEEM

SYSTEM DOWN
BEEEEP
HUH ?!
WHAT JUST HAP-PENED?!
WHIP
PSSHK
?

BLAM
BLAM
BTCHT
BTCHT
NKH ...!
WHO WAS THAT WOMAN ?!

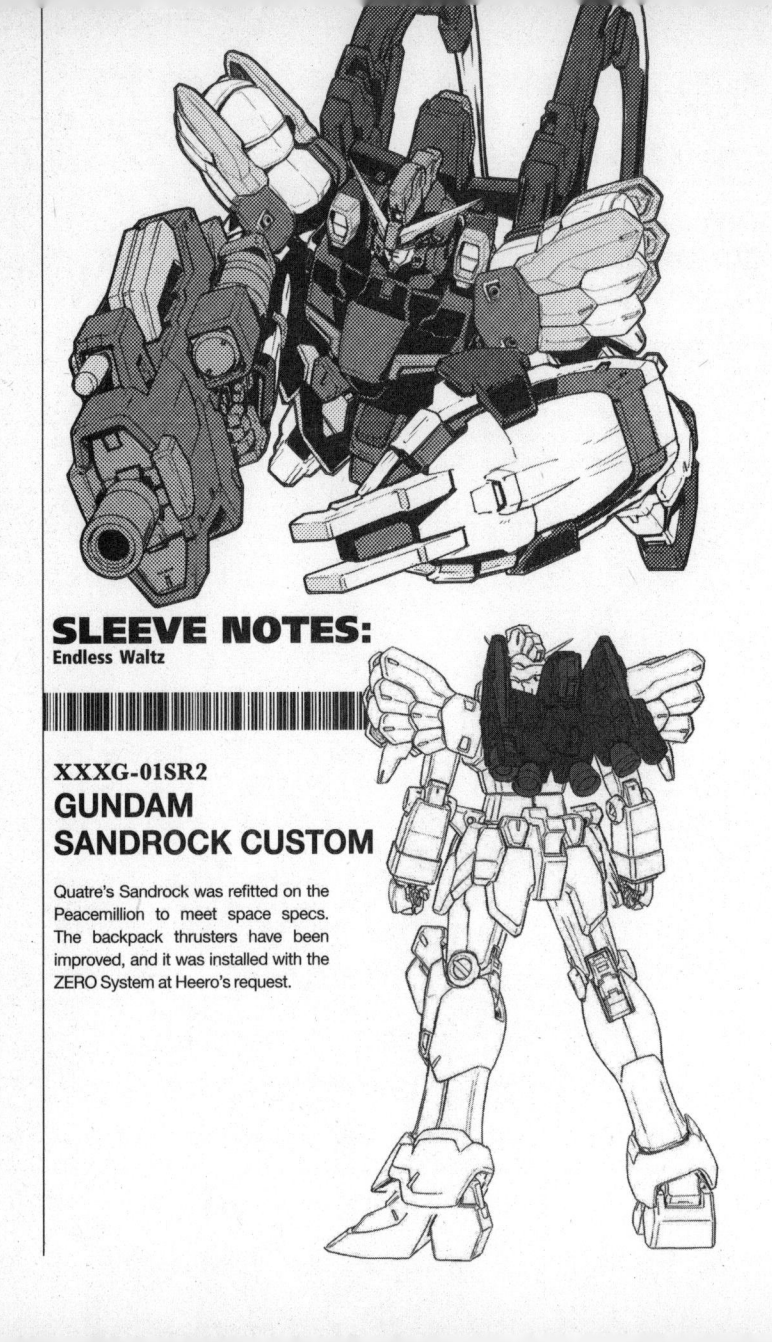

SLEEVE NOTES:
Endless Waltz

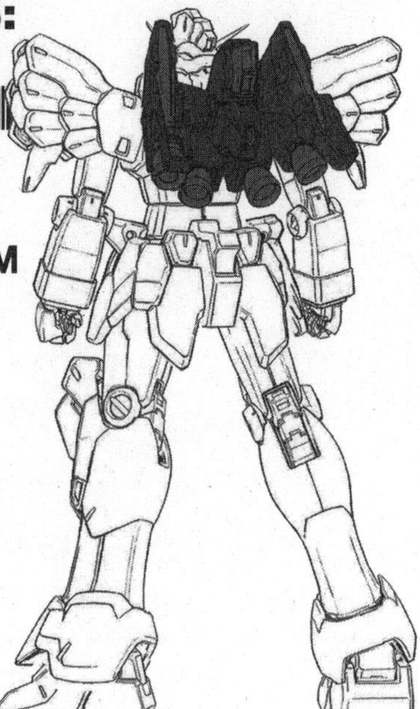

XXXG-01SR2

GUNDAM SANDROCK CUSTOM

Quatre's Sandrock was refitted on the Peacemillion to meet space specs. The backpack thrusters have been improved, and it was installed with the ZERO System at Heero's request.

SLEEVE NOTES:
Endless Waltz

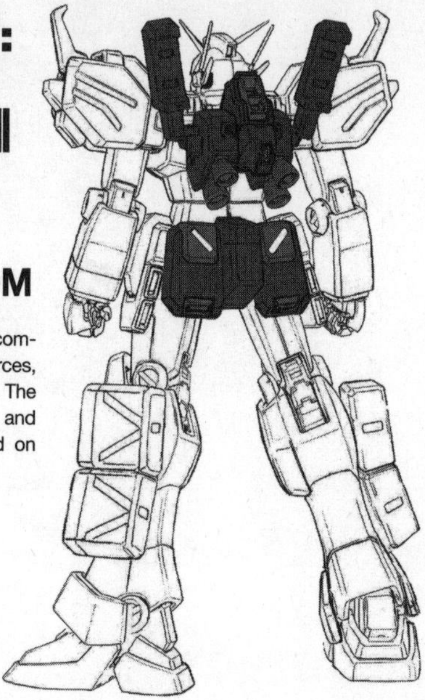

XXXG-01H2
GUNDAM HEAVYARMS CUSTOM

After the Heavyarms was badly damaged in combat with the OZ space military's remnant forces, Howard upgraded it to meet space specs. The backpack thrusters have been enlarged, and double Gatling guns have been mounted on each arm, amongst other improvements.

Chapter 78 "EVE WARS IV: The Sorrow of Space" Part 1

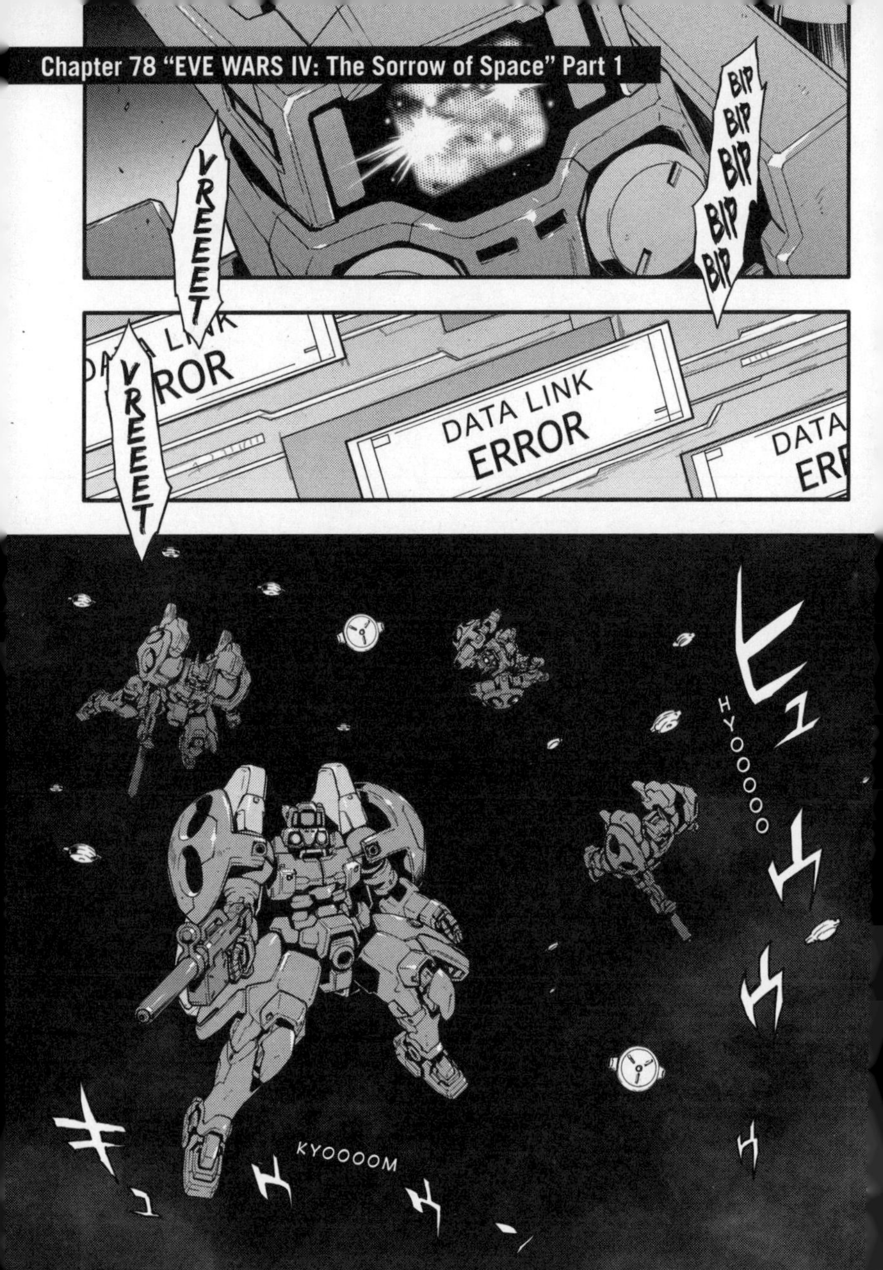

VWOMM
THE VIRGOS HAVE STOPPED MOVING ?!
OOOO
OOOOO
SO NOIN IS HERE ...
OOOO

I DON'T THINK THIS IS ENOUGH TO MAKE DOROTHY HESITATE ...

DWRRR
DON
DON
DON
DON
DON
NKH!
GWOOSH
BAMM
GYOOO

I'LL SHOW YOU...
JUST HOW DIF-FERENT WE ARE FROM THE MOBILE DOLLS!
VWWM
VWWM
VWWM
VWWM
VWWM
HMF!

BAMM
BAWHOOO
OOOO

GAKINK
GANK
BSHAK
DE-FEN-SOR MODE!!
DE-PLOY E FIELD!!
GYEEEEENN
VVWWOOAA

BSSHT
BAK
BAK
BAK
ZWA
HHSSSS

YOU ENDURED IT, EPYON. WELL DONE!
NOW WE CAN TEACH HIM THE WEIGHT OF SPACE'S RESOLVE!
GRAGINK
FINE.
LET'S SEE HOW MANY MORE BLASTS
YOU CAN TAKE!

BA
GRAA
OOO
OOO
BSSHT
ZHABAAM
BAASHT
OMM

ZZAT
ZZAP
ZZAAP
TCH ...!
FIRE ON ME ALL YOU WANT!
I CAN HANDLE ALL YOU'VE GOT, YOU'LL SEE!!

ZZWW
IF I CAN'T WITH-STAND THIS MUCH,
I CAN'T REPRESENT THE HEARTS OF THE PERSECUTED PEOPLE OF THE SPACE HABITATS!!
OMMM
...

MS. HILDE... THANK YOU VERY MUCH FOR HELPING ME,
BUT PLEASE LEAVE ME NOW.
PLEASE MAKE YOUR ESCAPE.
MISS RELENA, YOU DON'T UNDER-STAND.
THOSE OF US FROM THE COLONIES HAVE NOWHERE TO RUN TO.
HM ?
C-21

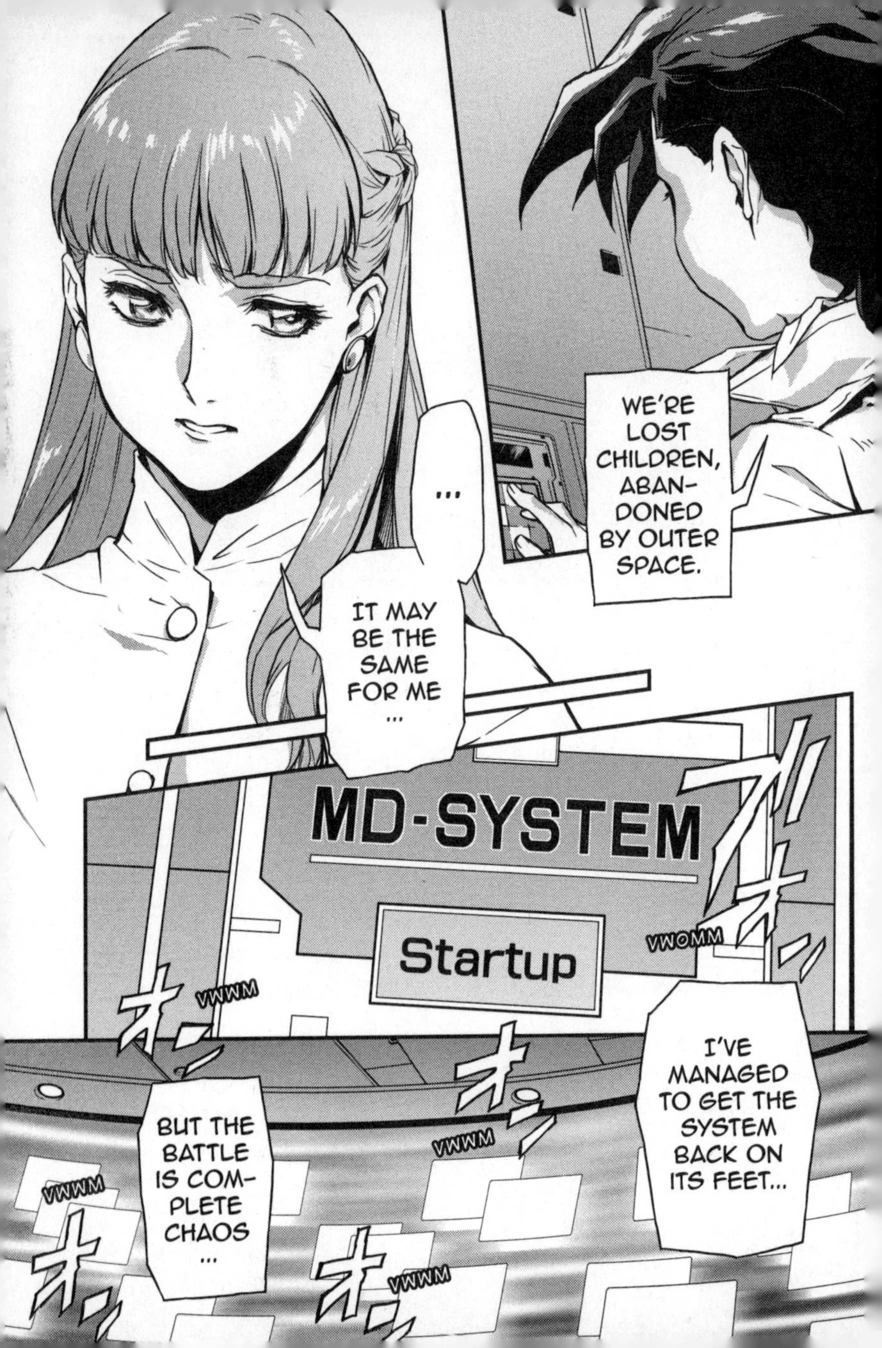
WE'RE LOST CHILDREN, ABAN-DONED BY OUTER SPACE.
...
IT MAY BE THE SAME FOR ME ...
MD-SYSTEM
Startup
VWOMM
I'VE MANAGED TO GET THE SYSTEM BACK ON ITS FEET...
VWWM
BUT THE BATTLE IS COM-PLETE CHAOS ...
VWWM
VWWM
VWWM

THERE ARE THREE ZERO SYSTEMS INTERVENING IN THE BATTLE!
THE WING ZERO, THE EPYON, AND A THIRD ZERO. IT'S CAUSING CHAOS.

DOOM
DOOM
DOOM
DOOM
DOOM
ZHABAM
BAWHOOM
I CAN SEE IT...
I CAN SEE THE ZERO'S FUTURE ...
THEY'VE BEEN ATTACKING US INDI-VIDUALLY SO FAR,
BUT THIS TIME, WE CAN USE THAT TO TURN THE TABLES AND DESTROY THEM ONE BY ONE.

WUFEI!
DUO!
CHARGE RIGHT INTO THEM AND DISRUPT THEIR BATTLE FORMATIONS!

RIGHT !
LEAVE IT TO US!
TROWA AND NOIN! FIRE ON THE SQUAD AT POINT 0-3-9 SIMULTA-NEOUSLY!
GOT IT!
ROGER THAT!

VWOOOOO
GWOOM
THE FLOW HAS CHANGED...
THEY'RE SURPASSING EVEN THIS ZERO'S FORECASTS...
JUST WHO IS THIS PERSON?
SOMEONE IS BEHIND THE MOBILE DOLLS...
WE'RE GOING TO FIND THEM!

TELL ME!
ZERO!
WHO IS HE ?!
WHO ARE YOU ?!
QUATRE RABERBA WINNER...
DOROTHY... CATALONIA...

FIRE THE LIBRA'S MAIN CANNON IMMEDI-ATELY!
WHPP
ZHFF
THE TARGET IS THE PEACE-MILLION!
DO IT NOW OR THE LIBRA WILL BE SUNK!
TH-THAT'S MAD-NESS!

VREEET
VREEET
MR. HOWARD! THE PEACE-MILLION NEEDS TO TAKE EVASIVE MANEU-VERS NOW!
THE LIBRA'S GOING TO FIRE ITS MAIN CANNON !!
WHAT DID YOU SAY ?!
DO YOU HAVE ANY IDEA HOW MASSIVE THIS SHIP IS?! IT CAN'T MOVE THAT NIMBLY!!
PUSH ENGINES 1 THROUGH 8 TO MAXIMUM OUTPUT! DISEN-GAGE LIMITERS AT THE SAME TIME!
IF WE DO THAT, WE'LL HAVE 360 SECONDS BEFORE ENGI-NEERING EXPLODES!

BETTER THAN GETTING SHOT DOWN!!
DO IT!
I'LL DEAL WITH THE ENGINES LATER SOMEHOW!!
FIRE THE MAIN CAN-NON?!
IF WE FIRE WHILE TRAVELING AT THIS SPEED, THE LIBRA WILL BE BLOWN APART!
FIRE! IT'S THE ONLY WAY!

GWOO
OOOO
?!
EMERGENCY!! A ZERO SYSTEM IS FORCING ITS WAY INTO LIBRA'S CONTROL SYSTEMS!
ERROR
ERROR
IT'S INFILTRATING THE MAINFRAME AND HACKING THE MAIN CANNON FIRING SEQUENCE!
I CAN'T STOP IT!
AAH...! I-IT'S TAKEN OVER COMPLETELY!!
NKH ...!
ASK COMMANDER MILLIARDO FOR THE ZERO HALT CODE!!

VWOO
OOO
MM
I DON'T HAVE THE POWER TO SHUT DOWN LIBRA'S MAIN CANNON!
BUT I HAVE TO TRY!!

QUATRE!
TROWA!
DON'T GET NEAR ME!
I'M GOING TO SELF-DESTRUCT THE SANDROCK AND NEUTRALIZE THE LIBRA!!

WH- WHAT ARE THESE IMAGES I'M SEEING ...?!
BAASHT
BAMM
GRA
GRA
AUGH!
GRA
GRA
NGH!

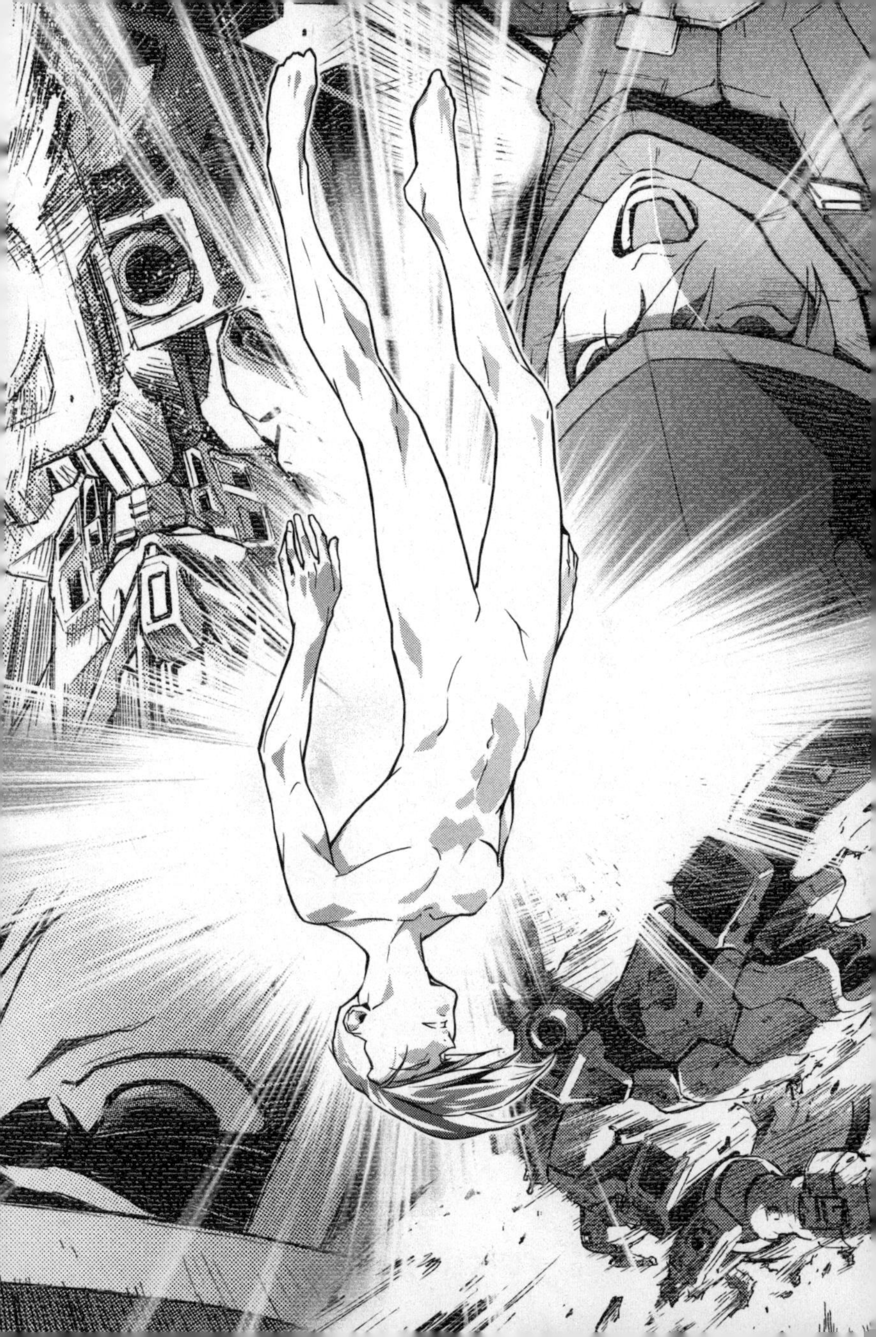

GABOOM
Q- QUATRE ...
YOU CAN'T ...

THIS ISN'T LIKE YOU!
HUH ?
TROWA ...?
YOUR MEMORY, IT'S...
YES ...
IT SEEMS TO HAVE COME BACK TO ME COM-PLETELY...

OH...
OHH...
QUATRE... YOU'RE SO KIND-HEARTED. IF YOU HURRY OFF TO YOUR DEATH, YOU'LL END UP LEAVING ONLY SADNESS BEHIND.
YOU WERE THE ONE THAT SAID WE HAVE TO KEEP ON FIGHTING OUR OWN HEARTS...
RIGHT?

XXXG-00W0

WING GUNDAM ZERO

SLEEVE NOTES:
Endless Waltz

ASTROSUIT

The astrosuit worn by Heero and the other Gundam pilots in the EVE WARS. They are tailored to fit their individual bodies.

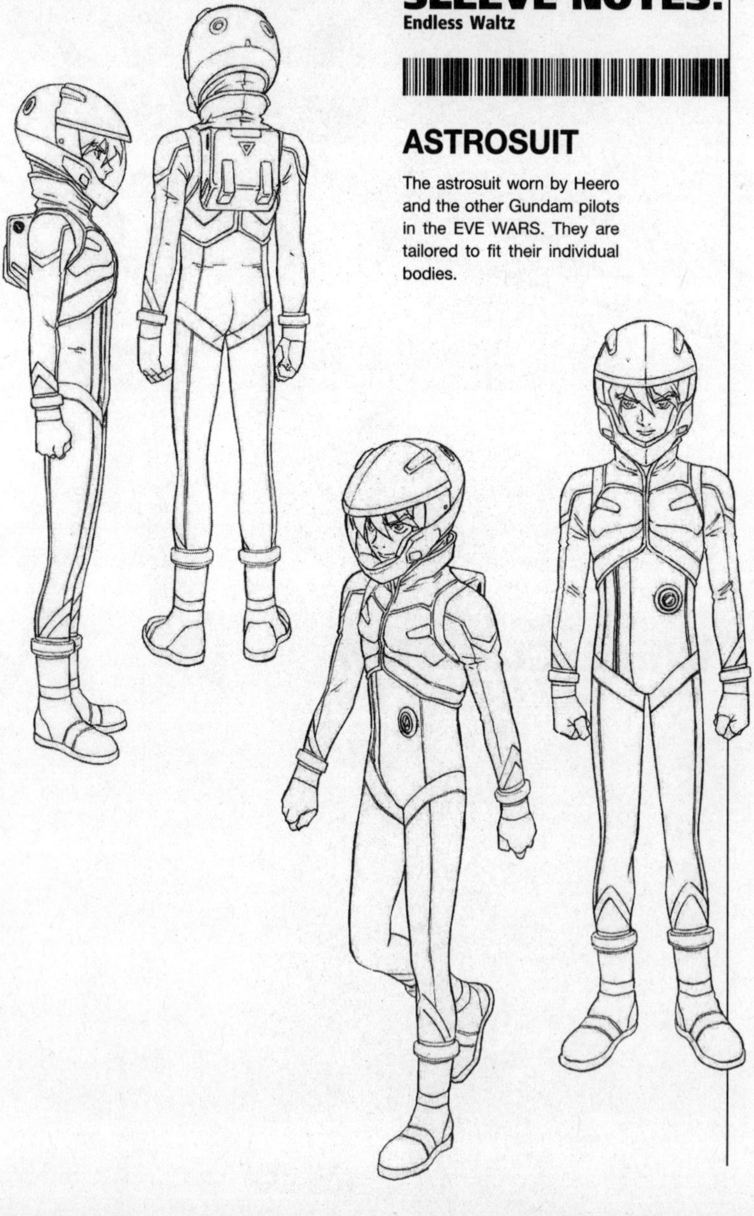

Chapter 79 "EVE WARS IV: The Sorrow of Space" Part 2

DON DON DON DON DON DON
THAT'S WHAT CATHRINE TAUGHT ME.
THANK YOU, TROWA ...
JUST HEARING YOU SAY THOSE WORDS MAKES ME OVER-JOYED.

VWOOSH
QUATRE !!

BAAM
BAASHT
KH...! SO IT WAS ALL TOO MUCH FOR DOROTHY, HM?
BIP
BIP
BIP
BIP
VREEET
MD SYSTEM
ERROR
VREEET

ZWAAM
ZECHS! TURN OFF YOUR ZERO!
VVM
SHUT DOWN THE SYSTEM!
THIS IS HARDLY THE TIME TO DO THAT!

ZECHS!
HEERO!
!

VOOSH
PSSHT
OUT OF THE WAY, NOIN!
NO! I'M NOT BUDGING!
GRNNK

VOOSH
GCHINK
BAKUNK
BSHAK
GRINK
ZWOOSH

HEERO!!
DAMN IT! GET OUT OF THE WAY, NOIN!
WHATEVER REASONS THERE MAY BE, YOU TWO MUSTN'T FIGHT!
WHAT THE HELL ARE YOU TALKING ABOUT ...
...
YOU'LL MAKE MISS RELENA SO SAD.

FIRE! SHOOT HIM DOWN!
THE HEAD OF THE GENERAL IS THE TROPHY TO GET !!
I'M NOT MOVING FROM THIS SPOT,
EVEN IF YOU KILL ME!!

VAWHOOSH

NKH!
GYOOOMM
DWOOM
DAMN IT!

GWOOSH
GANK
HOW COULD I BE SO SOFT ...?
DAMN IT!
...

The Earth.
A planet in the Solar system where life is miraculously able to thrive...
In A.C. 195, through the development of the colonies, humans became able to possess new lands thanks to their abundant resources and cultivation of technology.
However, this domain is never any more than an imitation of humanity's motherland, the Earth.

For what purpose were the colonies ever constructed?

It is said that the main objective was technological progress, in order to enrich the lives of mankind in the Earth Sphere. But was humanity coming to this imitation domain with impossible demands?
Out there, without the threats of nature, life has more stability than on the Earth.

It would appear that mankind had been promised eternal survival by development that knows no bounds. There must have been an age in which people were free to imagine they would be permitted to start afresh out there in space.
But it is difficult to believe that the colonies—no, humankind—could forget the Earth.

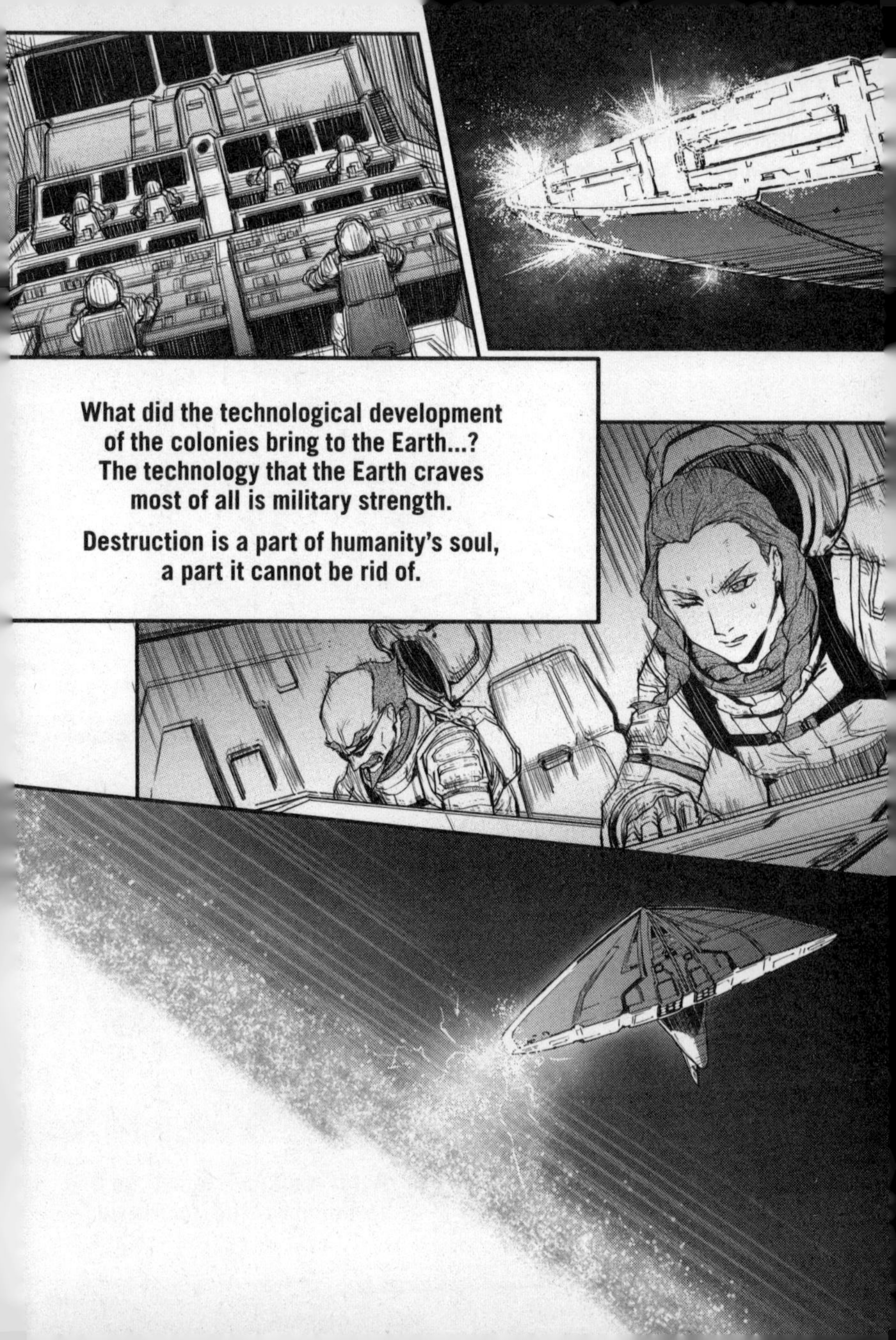
What did the technological development of the colonies bring to the Earth...? The technology that the Earth craves most of all is military strength.
Destruction is a part of humanity's soul, a part it cannot be rid of.

And now, the colonies have developed a militaristic temperament. They were unable to forget the Earth.
The Earth's beauty is grand.
Humankind, a species which has come to wield great power, is now thinking about the power to control a whole planet.
On a planetary scale, the existence of a lifeform is only momentary,
and it is secondary.
But in the end, humanity's thinking does not change.

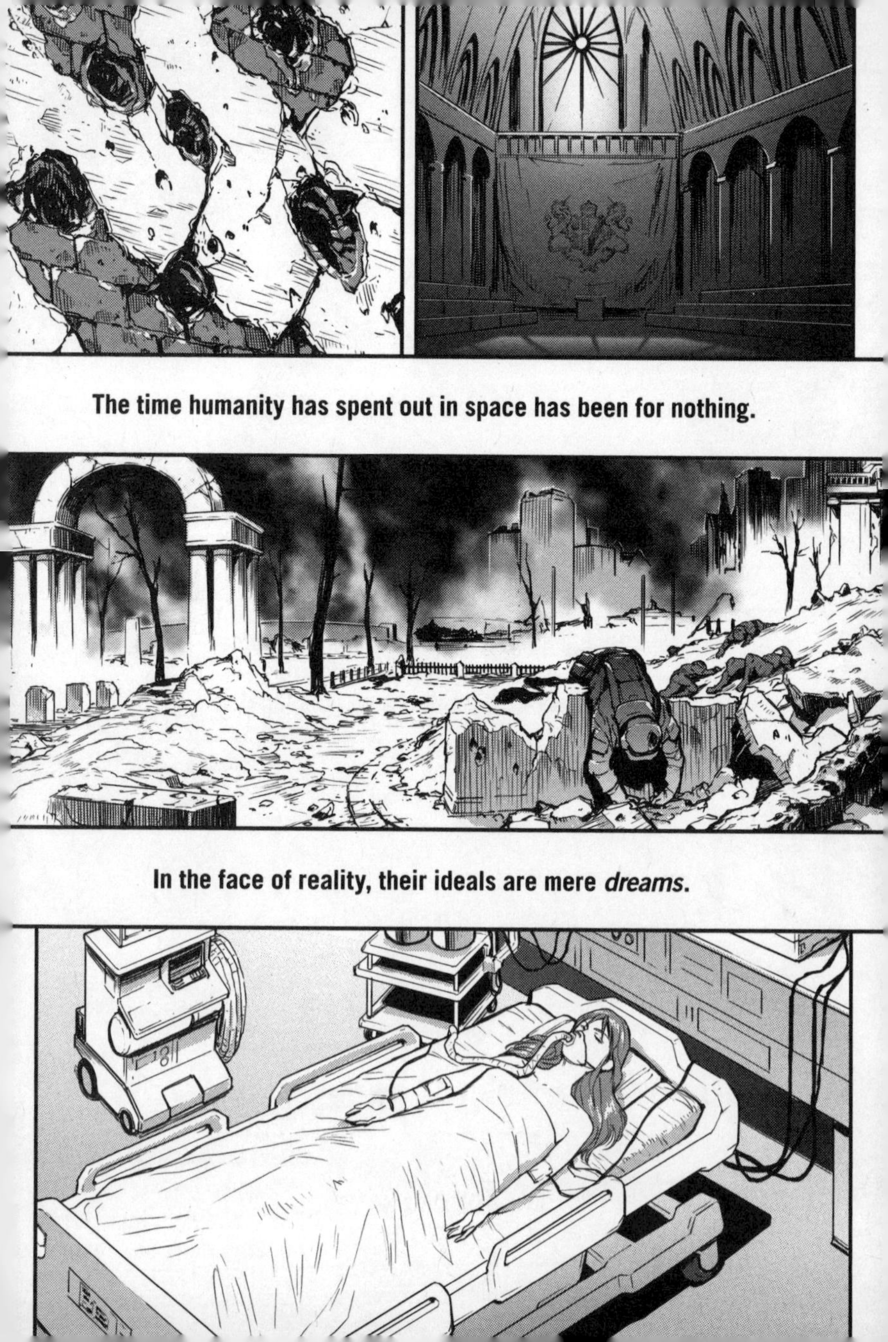
The time humanity has spent out in space has been for nothing.
In the face of reality, their ideals are mere *dreams*.

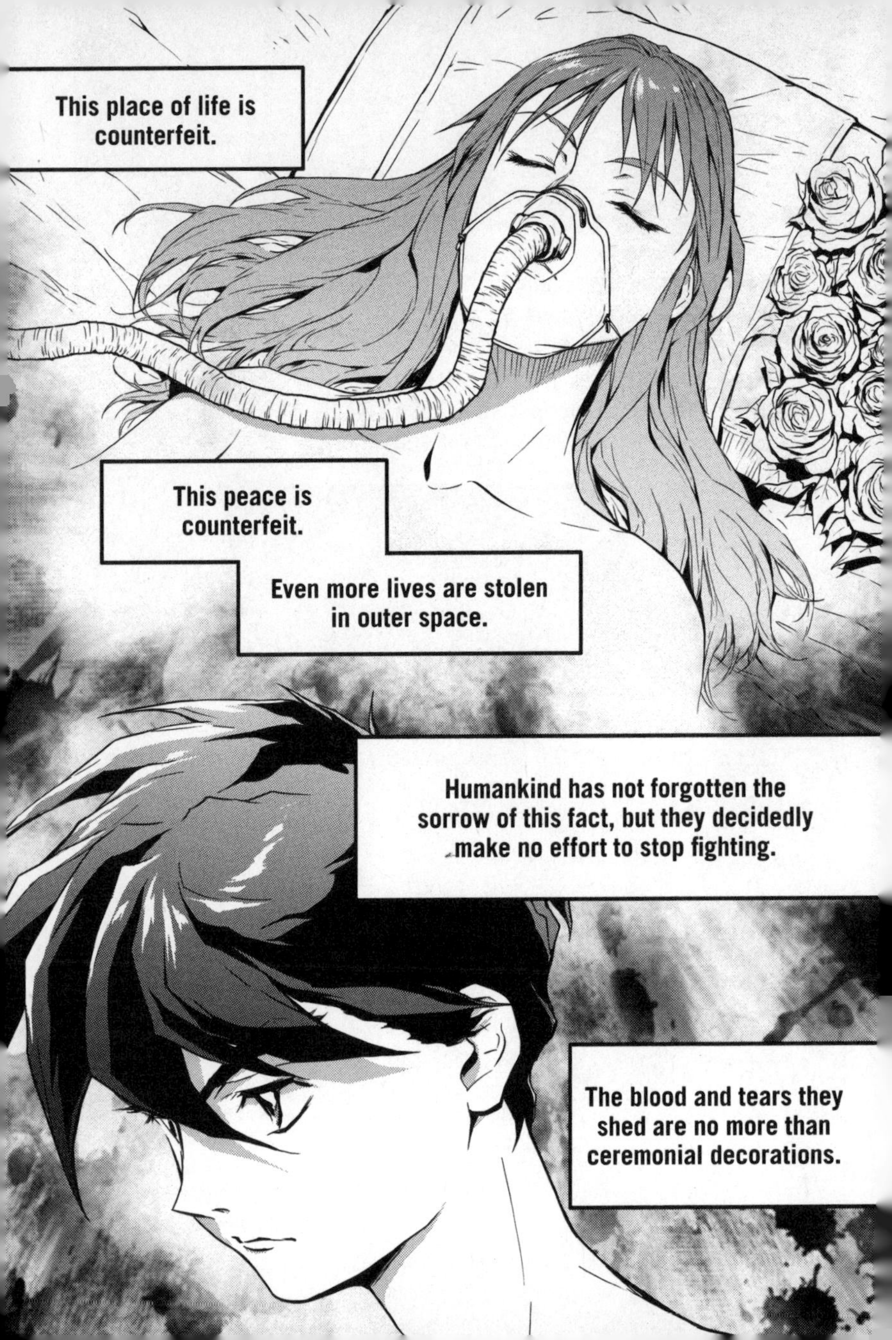
This place of life is counterfeit.
This peace is counterfeit.
Even more lives are stolen in outer space.
Humankind has not forgotten the sorrow of this fact, but they decidedly make no effort to stop fighting.
The blood and tears they shed are no more than ceremonial decorations.

There are histories in which the turning points can only be spoken of in terms of wars.
Faded, sugar-coated, twisted words about fighting for peace have been spouted over and over again.
For the sake of peace, the colonies took up arms and challenged the Earth.

No different from humanity on the Earth.
Much blood is spilled, and it heightens their fervor...

So why do humans fight? Perhaps the meaning of their existence lies in fighting.
Those who fight feel a sense of fulfillment.
And it is also a fact that those who fight are not seen as tainted.
To be continued...

Quatre *Raberba Winner &* **Trowa** *Barton*

SLEEVE NOTES:
Endless Waltz

XXXG-00W0

WING GUNDAM ZERO
Neo-Bird Mode

In the Wing Gundam Zero's Neo-Bird Mode, the shield locks into place for atmospheric re-entry mode. The twin Buster rifle attaches to each side of the shield (which becomes the fighter's nose).

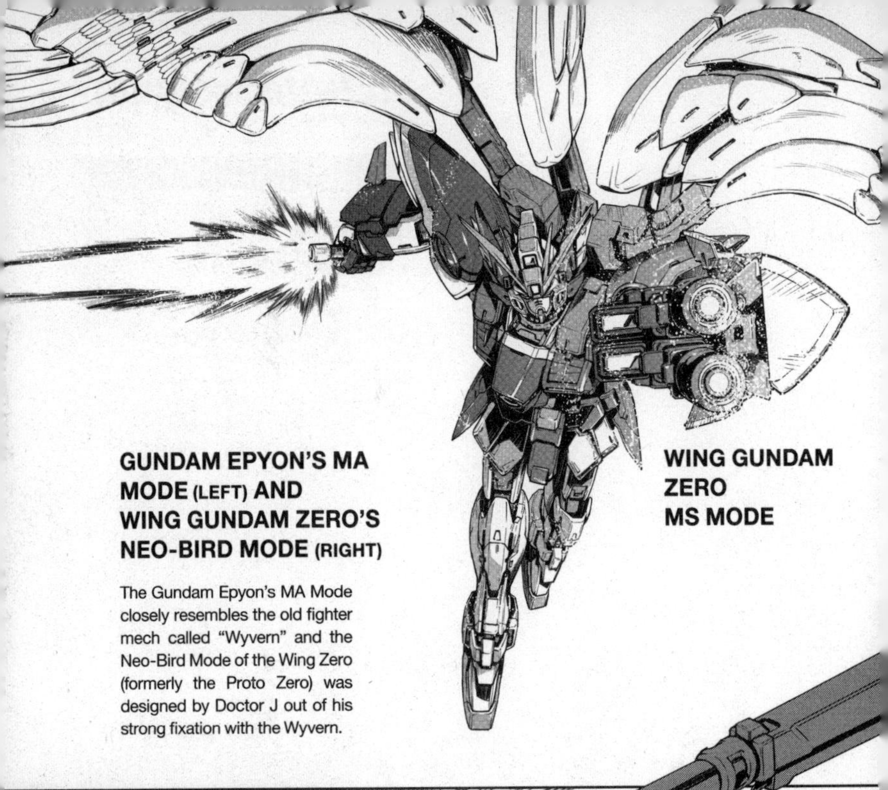

WING GUNDAM ZERO MS MODE

GUNDAM EPYON'S MA MODE (LEFT) AND WING GUNDAM ZERO'S NEO-BIRD MODE (RIGHT)

The Gundam Epyon's MA Mode closely resembles the old fighter mech called "Wyvern" and the Neo-Bird Mode of the Wing Zero (formerly the Proto Zero) was designed by Doctor J out of his strong fixation with the Wyvern.

SLEEVE NOTES:
Endless Waltz

OZ-00MS2
TALLGEESE II

The Tallgeese II was built out of remaining reserve parts. It has the same specs as Zechs's Tallgeese except for the face pieces, which resemble a Gundam. It is equipped with a Dober Gun, a Beam Saber, and an exclusive Heat Saber, among other armaments.

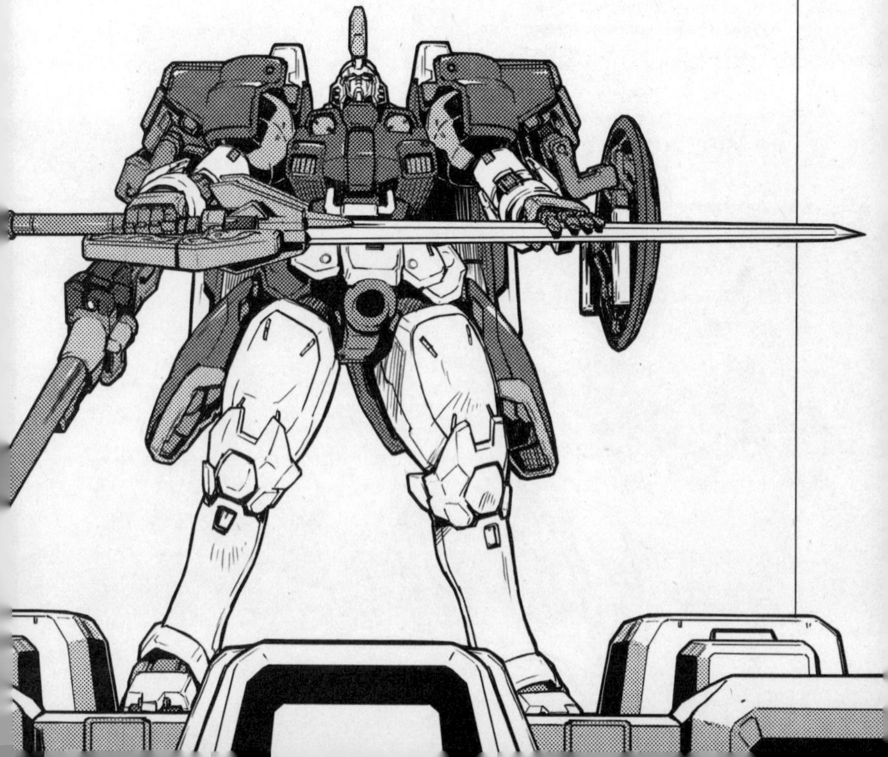

Mobile Suit
GUNDAM WING
Endless Waltz
Glory of the Losers

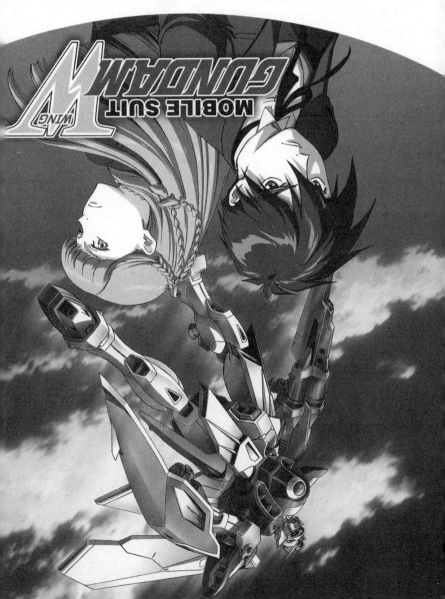

Mobile Suit

GUNDAM WING

Endless Waltz

Glory of the Losers

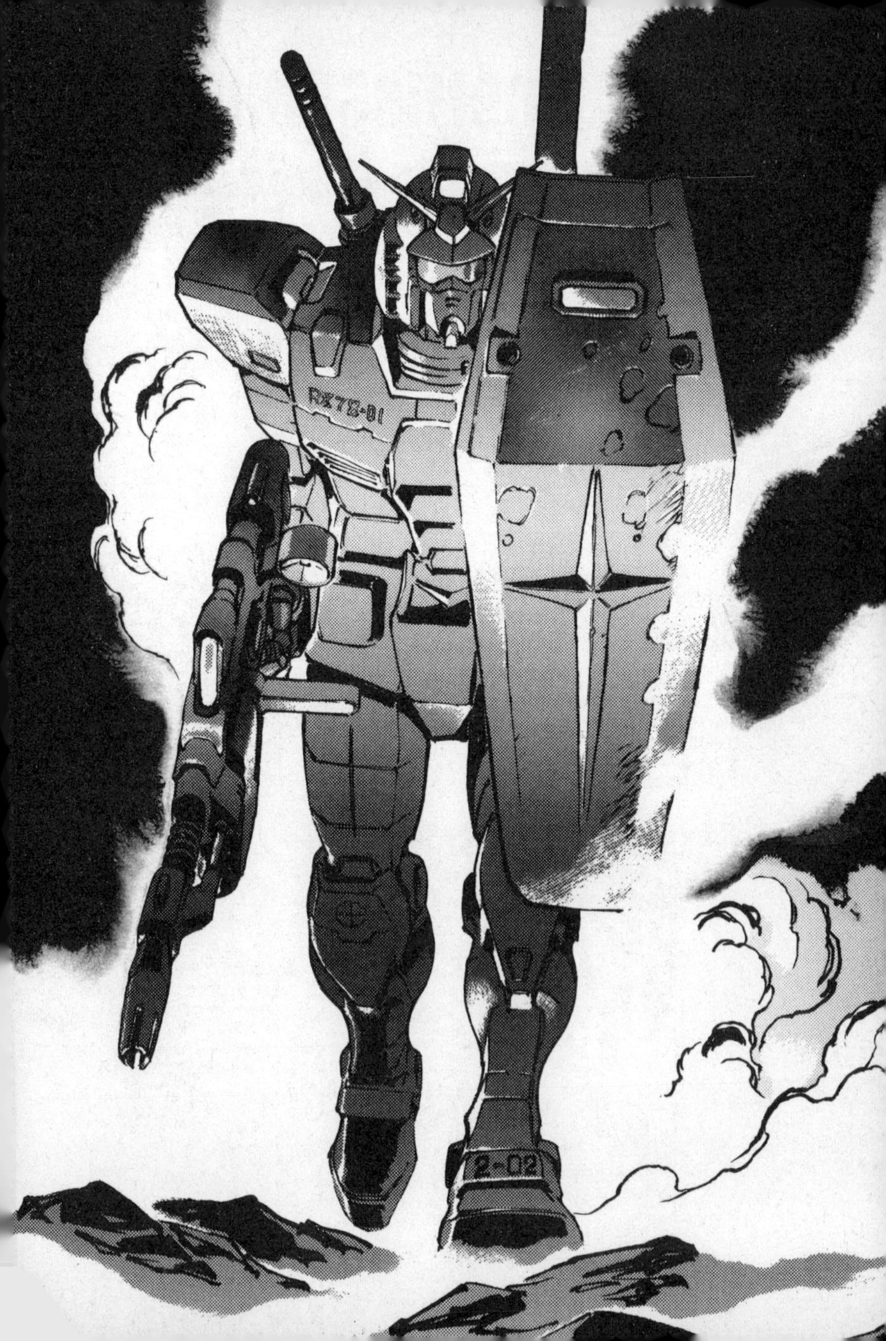
RX78-01
2-02

This story takes place on the frigid, massive artificial planet known as Aposimz.

Eo, Biko and Etherow, residents of the White Diamond Beam, are in the middle of combat training when suddenly a girl appears, Rebedoan Empire soldiers in hot pursuit. The girl asks for their help in keeping safe a "code" and seven mysterious "bullets." This chance encounter marks a major shift in the fate of the entire planet...

The curtain rises on a grand new adventure from Tsutomu Nihei, the author of *BLAME!* and *Knights of Sidonia.*

VOLUMES 1-3
AVAILABLE NOW!

APOSIMZ

TSUTOMU
NIHEI

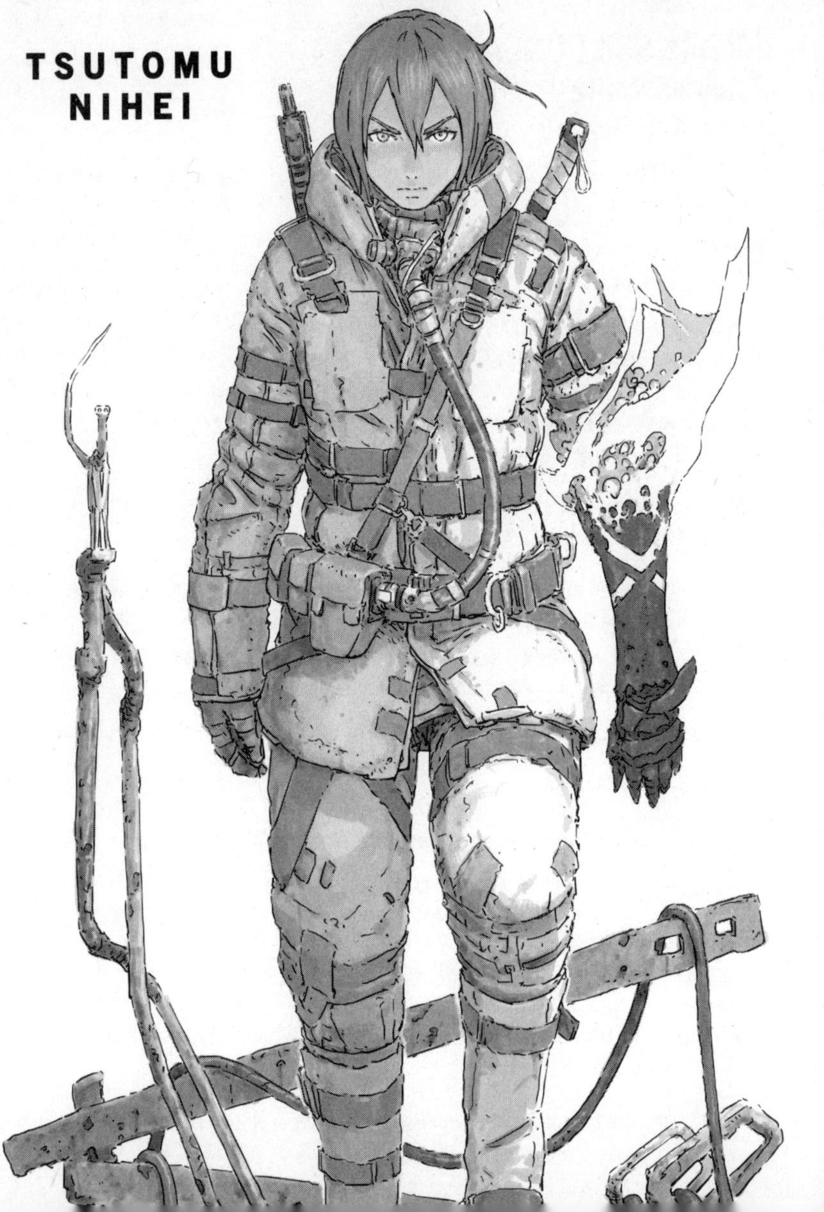

Mobile Suit GUNDAM WING, 13
Endless Waltz
Glory of the Losers

A Vertical Comics Edition

Translation: Kumar Sivasubramanian
Production: Grace Lu
Hiroko Mizuno

Translation provided by Vertical Comics, 2019
Published by Kodansha USA Publishing, LLC, New York

Originally published in Japanese as *Shin Kidou Senki Gandamu Wingu Endless Waltz The Glory of Losers 13* by Kadokawa Shoten, Co., Ltd.
Shin Kidou Senki Gandamu Wingu Endless Waltz The Glory of Losers first serialized in *Gundam Ace*, Kadokawa Shoten, Co., Ltd., 2010-2017

This is a work of fiction.

ISBN: 978-1-947194-65-6

Manufactured in the United States of America

First Edition

Kodansha USA Publishing, LLC.
451 Park Avenue South
7th Floor
New York, NY 10016
www.vertical-comics.com

Vertical books are distributed through Penguin-Random House Publisher Services.